CW01045326

HAROLD WILSON

ALSO BY ALAN JOHNSON

Memoir

This Boy
Please, Mister Postman
The Long and Winding Road
In my Life

Novels

The Late Train to Gipsy Hill
One of Our Ministers is Missing
Death on the Thames

HAROLD WILSON

Twentieth Century Man

ALAN JOHNSON

Swift

SWIFT PRESS

First published in Great Britain by Swift Press 2024

1 3 5 7 9 8 6 4 2

Copyright © Alan Johnson 2024

The right of Alan Johnson to be identified as the Author of this Work has been
asserted in accordance with the Copyright, Designs and Patents Act 1988.

Text design and typesetting by Tetragon, London
Printed and bound in Great Britain by CPI Group (UK) Ltd, Croydon CRO 4YY

Frontispiece: Harold Wilson smokes pipe
at Labour Party press conference, ANL/Shutterstock

A CIP catalogue record for this book is available from the British Library.

ISBN: 9781800753327
eISBN: 9781800753334

To Sue Utting, Watford's finest, who worked so diligently for Harold Wilson in Parliament and, thirty years later, for me.

PREFACE

HAROLD Wilson wasn't the first British Prime Minister to be born in the twentieth century. That distinction belongs to his Conservative predecessor. However, it is fair to say that Wilson was the first Prime Minister perceived as being of the modern age. The man he succeeded had been the Fourteenth Earl of Home (pronounced 'Hume'), before renouncing the peerage and becoming Sir Alec Douglas-Home. Often seen shooting grouse dressed in plus fours on his Scottish country estate, Douglas-Home seemed more Edwardian than new Elizabethan. As a member of the un-elected House of Lords, he had no democratic mandate. Worse still, as a hereditary peer, he occupied a seat in Parliament's upper chamber only because of the nefarious activities of his ancestors.

The contrast between the aristocratic Lord Home and plain Mr Wilson could not have been more distinct. It neatly reflected the early-1960s tension between ancient and modern Britain, as memorably described by the historian David Kynaston:

A world where the war was still fresh in the national memory, but where the end to post-war austerity meant that shopping was becoming a leisure activity; a world where homosexual relationships were still illegal, but where a new individualism in taste and identity was starting to emerge; a world where married women still mainly stayed at home and where divorce was still almost unthinkable, but where pop music was disrupting traditional cultural hierarchies and where there was a new impatience with what was now mockingly known as 'the Establishment'.

The poet Philip Larkin famously framed it as the period when sexual intercourse began: 'between the end of the *Chatterley* ban and the Beatles' first LP.'

That first album was released in March 1963, two months after Hugh Gaitskell died of lupus (a rare condition affecting the immune system). On 14 February, Labour MPs elected Harold Wilson to replace him. By then the Labour Party had been in opposition for almost 12 years, having lost three successive general elections.

The Conservative Prime Minister was Harold Macmillan, but in October of that same year, severely damaged politically by the Profumo scandal, he was hospitalised for a prostate operation and resigned his premiership on grounds of ill health. (Ironically, he was to live for another 23 years, to become the second-longest-lived Prime Minister in British history.)

The man who emerged from the Conservative ranks to replace him was Lord Home. 'Emerged' is the appropriate word, because the Conservative Party did not hold elections to decide its leader among either its MPs or its members. Instead, a conclave of grandees gathered in a discreet location while the British people waited to be informed as to whom these important chaps (there were no women) had decided should be their Prime Minister.

For Harold Wilson, Home was a political gift beyond anything he could have hoped for. The Fourteenth Earl personified Wilson's trenchant criticism of an establishment that was humiliating the country and holding back its advance. He labelled the new Prime Minister 'an elegant anachronism', describing his appointment as a counter-revolution: 'After half a century of democratic advance,' Wilson thundered soon after Home's elevation, 'of social revolution, of rising expectation, the whole process has ground to a halt with the Fourteenth Earl.' The attack was perfectly judged. The fully enfranchised, better-educated, less deferential population of the television age was less inclined to accept the imposed hierarchies of its ancestors.

The Conservatives were stung by Wilson's criticism, and Lord Home spent just four days governing the country from the Lords before using legislation, pioneered ironically by Labour's Tony Benn, to renounce his peerage. However, it would be a while before a by-election could be organised to allow the newly unennobled Alec Douglas-Home to enter the Commons in a safe Conservative seat. This hiatus produced an even greater democratic anomaly. For almost three weeks Douglas-Home was the only Prime Minister in Britain's long constitutional history not to have a seat in either the Commons or the Lords.

The United States had already elected its first President born in the twentieth century: a man who epitomised the determination of a new generation to sweep away the *ancien régime*. While Wilson, the President's elder by just one year, couldn't match the dazzling glamour of JFK, the British press was soon describing him as 'the British Kennedy'.

Apart from a brief introduction during Kennedy's time as a senator, the two men met only once, on 2 April 1963, when Wilson flew to Washington to fulfil an engagement originally arranged for Gaitskell. Wilson later described Kennedy as 'the most full-time an active President's been in this century'. Referring to the tradition in Britain of older men in their sixties becoming Prime Minister, Wilson pointed out that Kennedy 'shifted the whole idea to a younger generation'. The two men got on well, but the next general election in Britain was then still 18 months away, and given the Labour Party's habitual knack of losing elections it was by no means certain that its popular new leader would ever become Prime Minister.

These twentieth-century men never had the opportunity to work together as President and Prime Minister, but that had nothing to do with the electorate. Larkin's poem immortalised the release of the Beatles' first LP, but the second had a far more significant release date: 22 November 1963, the day the thirty-fifth President of the United States of America was assassinated.

1

JAMES Harold Wilson ended his life as Lord Wilson of Rievaulx, and it was at Rievaulx, a village in North Yorkshire (which Wilson pronounced 'Rivers'), that generations of Wilsons had worked the land, adding the occasional supplementary occupation to increase their income. Harold's great-grandfather, John, for instance, was the village cobbler. It was John who was to break with the family's agricultural tradition, lifting the Wilsons a few notches up the social class scale by moving to a salaried profession.

A vacancy had occurred for a new master at the workhouse in Helmsley, the market town closest to Rievaulx. The severe economic recession of 1837 had caused a significant surge in demand for workhouse places. It was only by living in such establishments that any kind of municipal assistance could be accessed. Originally, John Wilson took on the role to supplement his meagre income, but he came to see that while Helmsley Workhouse represented destitution for its occupants, it could provide him with a route to a more prosperous future. And so he became the first Wilson to hold public office.

Three years after John's recruitment at Helmsley, he and his wife, Esther, became master and matron of a workhouse in York, where they remained for 26 years. Not only was this a more secure occupation than working the land, it carried a pension, which Esther relied on when John died in 1881. John and Esther's son, James (Harold Wilson's grandfather), had been the last Wilson to be born at Rievaulx, eventually following his father's example but in a more radical direction. James not only left the land, he left Yorkshire – crossing the Pennines to be an apprentice draper in Manchester at the age of 17.

Continuing the Wilsons' upward social trajectory, James married Eliza Thewlis, whose father, Titus, while based in Manchester, employed over a hundred men at a cotton-warp factory 50 miles away in Huddersfield. Titus was politically active. His son Herbert (James's brother-in-law) was an alderman and became a Lord Mayor of Manchester. Under the Thewlis influence, James began to take an interest in politics, defining himself as a radical Liberal.

Jack Wilson, the eldest of James and Eliza's six children, took that radicalism to a new level by becoming Keir Hardie's election agent at Merthyr Tydfil in the 1900 general election. That was the year in which 126 trade unionists meeting under the auspices of the Trades Union Congress (TUC) had formed the Labour Representation Committee (LRC), with Hardie as its secretary. Six years later, the LRC renamed itself the Labour Party. Like a substantial proportion of the voting population, the Wilsons were gradually shifting their political allegiance from Liberal to Labour, and Jack's political activity was bound to influence his younger brother, Herbert – Harold Wilson's father.

Born in 1882, Herbert Wilson was by all accounts a kind and benevolent man, but he had a lasting regret. While remaining in education until the unusually late age of 18, he'd never achieved his ambition of going to university. Given that higher education was the preserve of a tiny, prosperous elite, this was hardly a failure, but it intensified the ambition he would harbour for his children.

Herbert went to Manchester Technical College, training to become an industrial chemist. In 1906, at the age of 23, he married Ethel Seddon, the daughter of a railway clerk. The Seddons were committed trade unionists. When William Seddon, Ethel's father, had been advised to move to a warmer climate to ease his chest infection, the family decided to emigrate to Australia. Ethel was by then engaged to Herbert and so stayed behind, but her brother (another Harold) became a senior union official in Kalgoorlie, Western Australia, where he worked on constructing the transcontinental railway.

As far as we know, Herbert Wilson never contemplated following the Seddons to Australia, but, in 1912, after two generations of living west of the Pennines, he took the Wilsons back to their Yorkshire roots – to Milnsbridge, a small town in the Colne Valley a mile from Huddersfield. Herbert had become the manager at a dye manufacturer, where he oversaw the complex process of fabric production: scouring, tentering, drying, milling, blowing, raising, cropping, pressing and cutting. It was dirty, dangerous work that was soon to develop a lethal offshoot.

When the First World War began in 1914, there was a surge in demand for coal tar, an important ingredient in the manufacture of explosives. The substance and its derivatives were used widely in the dyestuffs sector: indeed, the company Herbert worked for claimed to have been the first British manufacturer of TNT. What was undeniable was that while the Great War was killing the city's sons, the reliance on artillery bombardment was making Huddersfield one of the most prosperous towns in the country. Herbert was placed in charge of the explosives department, and two years into the war had his salary increased substantially. Herbert and Ethel, whose daughter, Marjorie, had been born in 1909, could therefore afford to have a second child. It was at 4 Warneford Road, Milnsbridge, Huddersfield, a rented three-bedroom house, that James Harold Wilson was born on Saturday, 11 March 1916. The Prime Minister at the time was the Liberal H. H. Asquith, another Yorkshireman, born just ten miles away from the Wilsons, in Morley. Few would have believed that a second Prime Minister could be born in such close proximity.

2

A YEAR after his son was born, Herbert Wilson became a homeowner, buying a larger, semi-detached house in a better part of Milnsbridge – 40 Western Road. As the war was ending, he also made a propitious move in the jobs market, returning to his profession as an industrial chemist but with a new employer, L. B. Holliday & Co., Britain's biggest supplier of dyestuffs. The wartime need for explosives was declining rapidly, but the dyestuffs industry was prospering. For a time, fortune smiled on the Wilsons. Four-year-old Harold ('James' had already been discarded in favour of his middle name) was enrolled at New Street Elementary School, where he was soon excelling academically. His prodigious memory became apparent by the age of six, when he could effortlessly reproduce entire pages of the textbooks he'd read, complete with their complicated lists of figures. He made progress at school despite rather than because of his first teacher, Miss Oddy, whom in his memoirs Harold described as being 'either an incompetent teacher or a sadist, probably both'.

Aged eight, he appeared in what was to become the most celebrated childhood photograph of a Prime Minister. Taken on the doorstep of 10 Downing Street in the summer of 1924, in short trousers, capped and tightly jacketed, Harold Wilson stands in front of the famous black-lacquered door he was destined to walk through as Prime Minister 40 years later. In capturing his alleged precocity, the photo helped build a myth about Wilson having an all-consuming ambition to be Prime Minister. But the London excursion only happened because Harold had been hospitalised to have his appendix removed and Herbert, anxious to give his son a treat while Ethel and Marjorie were away, placed him in the sidecar of his motorbike for a week of travel which included an overnight stay at a cheap bed and breakfast in London. In those days (until 1982), tourists could stroll into London's most famous cul-de-sac to pose for photos outside No. 10. It would have been perverse for Herbert not to have done what most visitors to London did. Ironically, the occupier at the time was Ramsay MacDonald, who led a minority Labour administration for nine months during 1924, thus becoming Britain's first Labour Prime Minister – the little boy on his doorstep that day would become the third.

Four years after the Downing Street photograph, Harold won a *Yorkshire Post* competition to eulogise his greatest hero in fewer than a hundred words. His subject was Robert Baden-Powell. Wilson was an enthusiastic Boy Scout in a family of Baden-Powell devotees. Begun in 1908, the Scouting movement was making an enormous impact, particularly in God-fearing, Nonconformist households like the Wilsons'. Herbert became a Scout commissioner, Ethel a Guide captain, and Harold's sister, Marjorie, dedicated most of her life to the cause.

At that stage of his life, if he hadn't chosen Baden-Powell, Wilson would probably have plumped for Billy Smith or another footballer from the brilliant Huddersfield Town team that won the FA Cup in 1922 and were then league champions for three successive seasons between 1923 and 1926. Harold attended the Leeds Road stadium for most home fixtures.

It was in the last of those league-winning years, just after the General Strike, that he was to embark upon a great adventure, spending six months in Australia. His mother took him with her when she travelled to see her father, Grandad Seddon, whom she'd been told was at death's door. For a woman to set off without her husband on such a long journey would have been a bold thing to do in the 1920s. The cost alone was prohibitive, even for middle-class families like the Wilsons. It was a demonstration of Herbert's enlightenment as well as his prosperity that he drove his wife and son to the London docks (in the Austin 7 that had succeeded the motorbike) for the long journey to Perth, Western Australia, on HMS *Esperance Bay*. When Harold eventually returned to New Street School, he chose to relate his experiences in a series of two-hour lectures which every class had to attend. He also sent articles on aspects of his adventure, such as 'My visit to a gold mine', to children's magazines, although none were published. The trip may have formed his lifelong interest in Commonwealth affairs. It was certainly responsible for the first stirring of his political ambition, since it enabled him to witness his Uncle Harold, the trade unionist who'd worked on the transcontinental railway, become an elected representative of the Legislative Council of Western Australia.

3

IN September 1927, 11-year-old Harold Wilson began his secondary education at Royds Hall Grammar School, having passed the County Minor Scholarship (a forerunner of the eleven-plus), as Marjorie had done seven years earlier. Both were beneficiaries of their father's resolve for his children to enjoy the educational opportunities he'd been denied. Marjorie was to become that rarity of the age, a university-educated woman, studying Chemistry at Leeds. After failing her finals, she switched to teaching, which, together with the Girl Guides, became her vocation.

Harold threw himself into the extracurricular activities available at Royds Hall, particularly drama and sport. What he did not appear to excel at particularly was schoolwork. Early reports referred more often to his indolence than to his erudition. Only one teacher disturbed this consensus, pointing out that young Harold shone at languages, even dabbling at one stage in Esperanto.

In his second year at the school the boys had to produce an essay under the heading 'Myself in 25 Years'. It's here that we detect the first evidence of an ambition to hold high political office, although in his contribution Wilson saw himself not as Prime Minister, but as Chancellor of the Exchequer. The essay even contained details of his first Budget, including the introduction of a tax on gramophones, which young Harold considered a frivolity for the idle rich. His focus on the Treasury was understandable given that his local MP, Philip Snowden, had been Chancellor in that first Labour government of 1924 (and was to occupy the post again when the party returned to power in 1929). Snowden was greatly admired by Herbert Wilson, and it was hardly surprising that this influenced his increasingly politically aware son.

Two disruptive events happened in quick succession during Harold Wilson's grammar school education. The first could have ended his life; the second had a profound influence on the course it was to take.

In 1930 he was part of a Scout troop camping in the Yorkshire countryside. Together with a pal, he visited a local farm offering fresh milk straight from the cow. Harold accidentally knocked over his friend's glass but drank his own, becoming one of the 12 unfortunates who developed typhoid from the unsterilised milk. Before the discovery of antibiotics, typhoid was a killer. Half of those infected in this outbreak died. Boy Scout Harold narrowly escaped the mortuary, but spent almost four months incarcerated at Meltham Isolation Hospital in a critical condition. A beefy, strapping lad, his weight plummeted to four and a half stone, and he would walk with a stoop for the rest of his life. As visiting times were restricted to half an hour a week, there were few opportunities to learn about what was going on at home. But the main news (about the second disaster to afflict the family) would have been kept from him for his own good.

When he was discharged, it could be kept secret no longer: Herbert Wilson had lost his job. A third of men in the Colne Valley were out of work and Huddersfield, which had been protected from the worst of the recession by the strength of its textile and engineering sectors, had finally fallen to the scourge of the age. At 48, Herbert had to finance the family from his savings, which led to a significant decline in their standard of living. His period of enforced idleness had a defining political influence on his son. Too young to understand fully his father's despair, Harold always regretted thoughtlessly asking for the three shillings and sixpence (17½p) he needed to buy a sheath knife. His father's awkward and disconsolate response – 'I can't just now, you know how it is' – was so seared upon his son's memory that it was recorded word for word in Wilson's memoirs.

The wonder is that these two significant setbacks did not have a more negative impact on Harold's education. Without his father's single-mindedness, he may well have been forced to leave school at 16 and contribute to the family income. The typhoid put him behind academically, but this would have been far more damaging were it not for the extra tuition given by his Maths teacher, who coached Harold in geometry and algebra free of charge after school. The teacher was a member of Huddersfield Labour Party, and so his influence was political as well as pedagogic.

This was a particularly turbulent period in Labour history. Philip Snowden (the Wilsons' MP) precipitated a crisis when, as Chancellor in MacDonald's second administration, he insisted upon a cut in unemployment benefit as part of a package of measures to counter the economic slump. The Cabinet refused to endorse Snowden's plan; the government collapsed, and when Ramsay MacDonald went to Buckingham Palace to tender his resignation, he was instead persuaded by King George V to return to Downing Street as head of a 'National Government' supported by the Conservatives and some Liberals. Snowden, as one of the few Labour ministers to join that government, was expelled from the party (along with MacDonald).

Herbert Wilson remained unemployed for 16 months and when he found work it was as chief chemist at Brotherton's Chemical Works on the Wirral. The Wilson family would need to relocate to Cheshire, and Harold would have to change schools at a critical point in his education. Wirral Grammar was a brand-new school for boys, whereas Royds Hall had been co-educational. Like all new schools it filled gradually as each cohort of 11-year-olds joined and the previous one moved up a year. When Harold arrived as a 16-year-old in 1932 he was the only sixth-form pupil, which meant the disruption of changing schools had the serendipitous effect of providing him with one-to-one tuition. His subjects were History, French and English (with Latin and Maths as subsidiaries). Despite his bout of ill health as a child he was also a keen athlete, excelling at long-distance running.

One sport that he had shown absolutely no interest in was tennis – until his first and hugely consequential visit to Brotherton's sports complex at Port Sunlight in 1934. Eighteen-year-old Harold had taken a break from revising for his Higher School Certificate (the equivalent of today's A levels) to watch his father win a bet.

Herbert Wilson had a party trick. Asked to multiply any two five-figure numbers he could do the sum in his head within 15 seconds. Upon hearing this, a disbelieving rival chemist at Lever Brothers placed a five-shilling bet that he could set a multiplication test that Herbert would fail. Herbert accepted the challenge, and Harold went to watch the contest. His father triumphed, but that wasn't what made the occasion so significant. After it finished, Harold wandered towards the tennis courts, where a shorthand typist by the name of Gladys Mary Baldwin happened to be playing. Eventually, like him, to be known by her second rather than first name, Gladys Mary had an immediate impact on her student spectator. Harold told a journalist many years later that it was love at first sight. Within a few days he had purchased a racket and joined the tennis club. Within three weeks, he'd told Mary of his intention to marry her.

What seems clear is that Mary was not as immediately smitten by Harold as he was by her. Two months older than him, she'd left school at 16 and was a working woman by the time she met schoolboy Harold. They shared the same Nonconformist background and worshipped at the same church, but these were the only things they had in common. Mary's father was a Congregationalist minister. Originally from Diss in Norfolk, the family had moved in accordance with her father's postings. At the puritanical end of the Protestant spectrum, Reverend Baldwin barred his daughter from reading novels and insisted that she attend church five times on Sunday. Her eventual escape from this regime was to a boarding school for educating the daughters of Congregational ministers in Crawley, Sussex. Despite her father's strictures, Mary developed a deep love of literature, particularly the poems of John Keats and Percy Bysshe Shelley and the novels of Jane Austen and Henry James. The one thing that Harold could never commit to his prodigious memory was poetry, and his artistic tastes were confined to the paintings of L. S. Lowry, Agatha Christie thrillers and the comic operas of Gilbert and Sullivan.

Harold may have declared his intention to marry Mary within a few weeks of their meeting but there would be no wedding for six years, a notably long engagement even by the customs of the time. All the evidence suggests that neither of them had any previous amorous relationships. Alone among his many biographers, Austen Morgan suggests that Harold had had one serious girlfriend before he met Mary. Apparently, her name was Doreen Richmond, and on their first date she was taken to see a film about the Congress of Berlin (which perhaps explains why there wasn't a second one). As for Mary, there is no indication of any previous suitors, but Ben Pimlott's fine biography of Wilson reproduces a poem she wrote about a schoolgirl's crush on a French mistress. The poem demonstrates a less puritanical Mary than her father would have wanted and a girl who may have entertained the occasional libidinous thought.

> My mouth is dry as she goes by –
> One curving line from foot to thigh –
> And with unEnglish liberty
> Her bosom bounces, full and free;

Pale skin, pink lips, a wide blue stare;
Her page-boy fall of silky hair
Swings on her shoulder like a bell;
O how I love Mamzelle!

Mary Wilson's poetry was to be a central feature of her future fame as the Prime Minister's wife, but she could never have expected to assume such a status with the lad from Huddersfield. By the time they married in 1940, the expectation was that Harold Wilson was destined for a career in academia, and there is little doubt that Mary would have been much happier there than in the harsh glare of British political life.

4

HAROLD Wilson had his sights set on a place at Oxford University, and meeting Mary didn't alter that ambition. He'd already applied unsuccessfully to six Oxford colleges when his father spotted an advert in the *Manchester Guardian* for an Open Exhibition in Modern History at Jesus College. Harold applied, obtaining the Open Exhibition but failing to win the scholarship, which meant that although he had secured a place at Oxford it was with a grant of only £60 per annum, whereas the scholarship had been worth £300, enough to cover annual fees and maintenance. His headmaster at Wirral Grammar pressured the local education authority to contribute £90 and Herbert agreed to provide the rest from his severely diminished savings.

Going away to university was a novel experience for Harold, whose only experience of living away from home, apart from hospital, had been at Scout camp. Jesus College lacked the glamour of Balliol or New College, where Labour contemporaries such as Denis Healey, Roy Jenkins, Richard Crossman and Hugh Gaitskell studied. And unlike them, Harold showed little allegiance to Labour while at university.

He did pay his half-crown subscription to the Labour Club, but rarely attended its meetings. It was chic to be a Marxist at the leading universities of the 1930s, and at Oxford a couple of hundred students who were Communist Party members had infiltrated the Labour Club. 'What I felt I could not stomach was all those Marxist public-school products rambling on about exploited workers and the need for a socialist revolution,' Wilson said years later.

It is inconceivable that Wilson could have studied economics without reading more of Marx than he claimed to have done. One presumes that his later comment about never getting beyond 'that whacking great footnote on the second page' of *Das Kapital* was made with tongue in cheek, although he was certainly no Marxist, distrusting the rigid dogma and anti-religious thinking of the Communists.

With so many public-school revolutionaries around, Harold must have felt fortunate to be sharing a room with the unpretentious son of a Welsh plumber from Tenby.

After exams at the end of the first term (known as 'Moderations'), Wilson took the crucial decision to switch subjects from Modern History to Philosophy, Politics and Economics (PPE). Known originally as Modern Greats, the subject had only been introduced in 1921 and was destined to pervade British political life. The college principal would only allow such a change if Wilson added a qualification in German to the French he already had. It seems a perverse requirement for a PPE student and the intention may have been to set Wilson up to fail, but if that was the principal's plan, it didn't work. Despite not speaking a word of German, and with only a self-help manual to guide him, Wilson studied hard throughout the six-week Christmas break, sat the exam and passed.

Politics at that stage was certainly an interest but not a passion. And where he stood on the political spectrum is a matter of conjecture. His Politics tutor could not tell if his pupil was Labour or Liberal, only that he wasn't a Tory. Wilson began attending meetings of the Liberal Club, even assuming office as treasurer. Such political cross-dressing on the left wasn't unusual at the time, and there were plenty of voters who were equally uncertain whether to place their anti-Conservative cross against the Labour or the Liberal candidate. While the Liberal Party was on the road to extinction as a governing party, they hadn't arrived there yet. At one time the favoured party in the minority of working-class households which had the vote, they failed to capitalise on Ramsay MacDonald's travails but continued to wield considerable influence through the *Manchester Guardian*, which was a liberal (and Liberal) newspaper. The *Guardian* had long been required reading in the Wilson household. The more congenial atmosphere of the Liberal Club must have been infinitely preferable to the vicious infighting of the various socialist factions over who could lay claim to ideological purity.

Wilson's involvement with the Liberals, never strong, had petered out by his second year, and in the run-up to his finals he made his allegiance clear by aligning himself with Labour, not through any of the various student affiliations, but by joining the local Oxford constituency party, where the diverse membership was more to his taste. By this time, he was well on the way to becoming the outstanding student of his generation. It wasn't just that he secured the top First Class Honours of his year or the first ever alpha-plus in economic theory: what made his academic achievement so outstanding is that he did all of that at the same time as acquiring a brace of glittering prizes.

The Gladstone Memorial Prize at Oxford University was (and still is) a major distinction. In 1936 *The Times* announced that it had been awarded to 'J. H. Wilson, Exhibitioner of Jesus College' for his essay 'The State and the Railways in Great Britain 1823–63'. Harold claimed to have had to read more than 300 books to produce the 18,000-word essay, which included 400 footnotes. As well as being an achievement of great academic merit, it carried an award of £100 (worth 87 times that today) and a prize oration in the grand surroundings of the Sheldonian Theatre. Harold's parents came to hear his speech, bringing with them an admiring Gladys Mary Baldwin, still the brilliant student's girlfriend, though yet to become his fiancée.

Rather than rest on this enormous laurel, Wilson set his sights on the George Webb Medley Junior Economic Scholarship, which provided a two-year postgraduate opportunity at £300 a year. He added this to his achievements before concentrating on his brilliantly successful finals (known at Oxford as 'Schools'). So, from 'Moderations' to 'Schools', Harold Wilson's time at Oxford was marked by high achievement. The Webb Medley scholarship would allow him to remain, at least temporarily, in academia.

Away from the dreaming spires, Europe was in turmoil. The turbulence that had begun with the Russian Revolution in 1917 had unleashed countervailing forces of totalitarianism that had already led to a Fascist government in Italy under Mussolini in 1922. Hitler's Nazis seized power in Germany the year before Harold went up to Oxford, and Franco ousted the elected government of Spain the year before he came down. In Britain, the 1935 general election had left the National Government in power but led by a Conservative (Stanley Baldwin). Labour, under 'caretaker' leader Clement Attlee, had at least improved on its dismal 1931 performance, but the party remained a long way from power. Due to the advent of the Second World War, there would not be another general election for a decade, and by then the name of the former civil servant whom Wilson went to work for next would be synonymous with the more compassionate post-war world he helped create.

5

IN 1937 William Henry Beveridge returned to his alma mater as master of University College, Oxford, after 18 years at the London School of Economics (LSE). He had a deep interest in all aspects of unemployment: how it had become so deeply ingrained in otherwise sophisticated and prosperous economies, its effect on society, and how to prevent it or at least alleviate its consequences. Having written what was already regarded as the classic text on the subject in 1909, he was now planning a sequel. Upon returning to Oxford, he asked some of his colleagues if they could recommend a capable research assistant. They could. Harold Wilson was not just the brightest graduate anyone could remember having at the university, he was noted for his love of statistical analysis. And he was available, thanks to the two-year postgraduate Webb Medley scholarship.

Wilson had applied for several positions before and after taking his finals, failing to become a journalist at the *Manchester Guardian* or a lecturer at All Souls. Helping Beveridge determine how society could be better ordered to ensure full employment (which Beveridge defined as an unemployment rate below 3 per cent) was an attractive proposition. This wasn't the report that made Beveridge's name, but it had some influence on what followed. Ironically, it was around this time that Herbert rejoined the dole queue, having lost his job at Brotherton's. Herbert would remain out of work for 18 months before finding a position at an explosives manufacturer in Liskeard. Just as combustibles had become Herbert's speciality in the First World War, it was to this sector that he returned as the Second World War approached. The 300-mile journey from one peninsula (the Wirral) to another (the Lizard) was the last great upheaval in the Wilson family chronicle. Harold's sister Marjorie took a teaching position in Cornwall and moved with her parents. While Harold didn't do that, he and Gladys Mary spent long enough at his parents' new house to develop a lifelong love of Cornwall and the Isles of Scilly, 28 miles off its coast.

Working for William Beveridge was far from lucrative. Beveridge couldn't even afford to pay a salary at first, only expenses, so Wilson had to find paid work elsewhere. Once again, what could have been a setback turned out to be advantageous. The work he found was a lecturing job at New College, which gave him the status of an Oxford don at the tender age of 21 and earned him an additional £125 a year plus full dining rights at the college. But a far more beneficial consequence was that his role was to support the senior economics lecturer, the hugely influential Labour figure G. D. H. Cole. It was Cole's thoughtful democratic socialism that helped his new understudy overcome a basic distrust of Labour Party intellectuals and attend the Oxford University Labour Club for the first time. This was when Wilson began to think seriously about a career in politics. Although Mary always insisted that it was her husband's intention to establish himself professionally as a don before even thinking about standing for Parliament, circumstances would set him on a different trajectory. After two terms teaching with Cole, Beveridge was able to turn Wilson's unsalaried part-time role into a full-time junior research fellowship worth £400 per annum. It was in this capacity that Wilson had to present a paper prepared with Beveridge to a meeting of the British Association for the Advancement of Science in Dundee. On the journey to Scotland Harold Wilson heard the news: Germany had invaded Poland; Britain was at war.

After making his presentation, Wilson headed back south to register at the Oxford labour exchange for war work or call-up as required by the Military Service Act. He broke his journey to spend a day with Mary and her family at Reverend Baldwin's latest posting in Penrith, and here the couple declared their intention to marry. Given that they had been committed to one another for five years and formally engaged since 1938, it was hardly a snap decision.

The wedding took place in the chapel of Mansfield College, Oxford, on a foggy New Year's Day, 1940. Both bride and groom were nursing bad colds as they set off for a short honeymoon at a Cotswolds hotel. Beveridge, still to assume national prominence, could not make the wedding but sent two red Venetian glass bowls as a present.

Arthur Greenwood, Labour's deputy leader and the minister responsible for reconstruction and post-war planning in the wartime coalition, would ask Beveridge to head up an interdepartmental committee on the coordination of social

29

insurance. This uninspiring template led to the most popular and influential document published by any government before or since.

The *Social Insurance and Allied Services* report quickly acquired the name of its author. Popularised in magazines such as *Picture Post*, the 'Beveridge Report' became central to the determination of the British public not to return to the austerity of the 1930s. When it was published on the day of Harold and Mary's second anniversary, a large queue formed outside His Majesty's Stationery Office in Kingsway, where 60,000 copies of the report, at two shillings (10p) apiece, were sold on the first day alone. Sales had reached 100,000 by the end of the month.

Beveridge's plan was designed to smite what he termed the 'five giants' of Want, Disease, Ignorance, Squalor and Idleness. Based on an assumption that there would be a National Health Service, and that the educational reforms drawn up by the coalition government would be implemented, Beveridge set out a contributions in return for benefits plan to create a welfare state that would protect its citizens from the cradle to the grave. The BBC World Service broadcast details of the plan in 22 languages. It was circulated among the armed forces as well as being exported to the United States, where Beveridge's work attracted great interest. Copies were parachuted into France and distributed throughout Nazi-occupied Europe. A copy of the Beveridge Report is said to have been found in Hitler's bunker.

Its inspiring message crossed the political divide in Britain, appealing to the left through its blueprint for social security and the eradication of poverty, and to the right for its emphasis on contributions in exchange for earned benefits. Shortly after the report's publication, its author told Wilson (with characteristic modesty) that it represented 'the greatest advance in our history. There can be no turning back. From now on Beveridge is not the name of a man; it is the name of a way of life, and not only for Britain, but for the whole civilised world.'

Few would have argued with that assessment back then, and many would still share it in these more cynical times. Its success must have caused Wilson to regret rejecting his former employer's invitation to act as secretary to the inter-departmental committee from which the report emerged. Little of Wilson's work on the impact of the trade cycle on unemployment levels was relevant to *Social Insurance and Allied Services*, although it did influence Beveridge's 1944 study *Full Employment in a Free Society*. Instead of accepting Beveridge's offer, which would have strongly associated Wilson with a document that helped change the world, he was allocated a temporary Grade 3 civil service clerical position – at the Oxford office of the Potato Control Board.

Beveridge was not the only historic figure to employ the youthful Oxford don. A professor at Newcastle University had been seconded to the Cabinet Office as economic advisor to Jean Monnet, chair of the Anglo-French Coordinating Committee. Monnet needed a research statistician, and the professor remembered the skilful presentation he had heard a few weeks earlier in Dundee. Harold was rescued from the Potato Board to be appointed to a position that lasted barely a month. The German invasion of France in May 1940 made advising Monnet on trade and supply routes a redundant task, but the modest French technocrat would go on to work with Robert Schuman to create the European Coal and Steel Community, forerunner of the European Union. It is why he is still regarded as 'the father of Europe', and why the joke among Eurosceptics is that Monnet is the root of all evil.

By the age of 25, Harold Wilson had worked for two of the most visionary and celebrated administrators of the twentieth century. While he and Beveridge became firm friends, it is doubtful that Wilson even met Monnet in 1940. However, we do know they met 34 years later, at the time of Britain's first referendum on Europe, when Prime Minister Wilson was said to hold the destiny of the Continent in his hands. As for the Cabinet Office job with the Anglo-French Coordinating Committee, it may have been of limited duration, but it brought the lad from Yorkshire to work in Whitehall for the first time.

6

HAROLD Wilson had a good war. Having briefly been an academic and then a civil servant, either profession could have become his calling. However, the academic work with G. D. H. Cole, combined with assisting Beveridge and Monnet, had only served to whet his appetite for politics and a career in Parliament – as a Labour MP. In 1943 he was invited by the Fabian Society to put his name forward for a place on their executive committee, a request obviously inspired by Cole, a Fabian luminary. As one of Labour's founding institutions (and the creator of the LSE), the society, dedicated to building socialism through a gradualist rather than revolutionary approach, exercised a power and influence greater than its size. In that same year, they put Wilson's name forward to Labour's headquarters as a potential parliamentary candidate, although by then he had attracted many other influential admirers. After his stint on spuds and a month working for Monnet, Wilson had been moved to the 'Manpower, Statistics and Intelligence' branch of the Board of Trade to work on fuel.

The supply of coal was crucial to the war effort. Government was worried that not enough was being produced, but the chaotic organisation of an industry with significantly more than 1,000 private companies owning almost 2,000 mines made accurate information difficult to establish. Wilson's initial job was to ensure that reliable statistics on coal output were available. He was a round peg in a round hole, finding genuine fascination and even excitement in the compilation of statistics. (Many years later, he became president of the Society of Statisticians, claiming that he'd recite the position to himself as a method of determining whether he'd had too much to drink.)

The colliery owners claimed that the main problem with maintaining output was that miners were taking too much time off. In a paper entitled 'Absenteeism and Productivity', Wilson identified far more profound issues around pay and conditions, which were compounded by the sprawling mess of so many individually owned mines.

Following a rash of strikes in the sector despite wartime legislation against industrial action, a Board of Inquiry was established under Lord Greene, with Wilson appointed as one of its secretaries on the strength of his well-received paper. A central grievance of the miners dating back to the General Strike of 1926 was the removal of a minimum wage, which left earnings entirely dependent on the amount of coal produced. Such was the reputation that 'Absenteeism and Productivity' acquired that Greene consulted Wilson, still a very junior civil servant, on this hugely controversial issue. The young secretary to the board was able to demonstrate how a minimum wage could be reintroduced without disturbing pay differentials or being prohibitively expensive. The Board of Inquiry recommended accordingly, and as a result Wilson's reputation spread.

Another recommendation of the board was that ministerial responsibility for the mines should shift from the Board of Trade to a new Ministry of Fuel, Light and Power. Wilson was appointed to be its first director of economics and statistics with a staff of 350 and a salary of £1,150 a year. Hugh Gaitskell, another Oxford graduate and ten years Wilson's senior, was working at the Board of Trade. He'd singled out Wilson as 'extraordinarily able', citing the way he had revolutionised coal statistics and insisting that 'we must on no account surrender him to the army'.

The government had been determined to learn from the experience of the previous war, when much administrative talent had been conscripted to the forces. There wasn't the same 'white feather' stigma this time, although conscientious objectors were still given a hard time. Harold Wilson wasn't a 'conchie': he had been perfectly prepared to fight for his country, and being a civilian in London wasn't without its dangers. Harold had a couple of narrow escapes. When he was sleeping at the ministry one night, the room next to his was destroyed in an air raid. On another occasion, a more devastating explosion wrecked the entire ministry. Fortunately, the director of economics and statistics was fire-watching elsewhere.

In the main, the Wilsons' domestic life passed peacefully enough, since they lived in less central areas of London, such as Richmond-upon-Thames. Here, according to one early biographer, Mary 'devoted herself once more to keeping a comfortable home for her hard-working husband'. That may have been the role expected of the 'housewife' of the 1940s, but Mary was not stereotypical. She volunteered to be an ARP shelter warden, which involved being on the streets in a tin hat when the bombs were falling, checking gas masks and ushering people to safety. Almost 7,000 wardens were killed during the war.

In September 1943 Mary gave birth to Robin, the first of the Wilsons' two sons. Thereafter, mother and baby lived mainly at Mary's parents' retirement home in Duxford, Cambridgeshire, although this was not entirely without risk given the village's proximity to one of the airfields from which the Battle of Britain had been fought.

In December, a few months after Robin's birth, Harold had lunch with William Beveridge, by now a great national figure. Harold wanted Beveridge's advice on the plan he was formulating to stand for Parliament as a Labour candidate at the earliest opportunity. Beveridge himself was considering a request from Labour to apply for the London University seat. To emphasise the residual Lib–Lab conundrum many were experiencing during this transformative stage in Britain's essentially two-party system, Beveridge rejected Labour and went on to win Berwick-upon-Tweed for the Liberals in a by-election the following year (only to lose it to the Tories in 1945). And Wilson's ministerial boss at the new Ministry of Fuel, Light and Power was Gwilym Lloyd George, the Labour-supporting son of the last Liberal Party MP to serve as Prime Minister.

Beveridge was unequivocally in support of his former

assistant's political ambitions but warned that he'd need to move fast given that the decision as to when to call a general election was exclusive to the Prime Minister and there was much speculation that Churchill would go to the country as soon as the war was over.

The Labour Party election machine, moribund since 1935, was cranking into life. The Fabian Society, having nominated Wilson for their executive, had also put his name forward to Transport House (the party HQ) for consideration as a candidate. With more names being submitted every day, the party's executive constructed an 'A' list consisting of candidates with trade union sponsorship, and a 'B' list of worthies without union support.

Mary, convinced that her husband would return to the academic world she loved when the war was over, wasn't unduly worried. Harold was 'B'-listed, and so less likely to be adopted. And his tender age would be a further obstacle: the British public preferred their MPs to be of a certain vintage. Even if nominated, he wasn't likely to defeat a Tory given that the Conservatives were bound to benefit from Churchill's enormous popularity.

Harold himself must have had his doubts. While not lacking in confidence he would have been aware that the majority of those being adopted by constituencies as Labour candidates had a track record of involvement in grass-roots politics: they would have served as constituency officials, attended endless meetings in draughty church halls, stood on countless doorsteps arguing Labour's cause. If they were not trade union officials, they would have an impressive war record. Many would tick both boxes.

None of this applied to Harold, but he did have a major advantage that few could match – his association with the miners. Wilson's work on countering the mine owners' arguments on absenteeism and re-establishing a minimum wage in the coalfields had not gone unnoticed. All the expertise he'd acquired on 'King Coal' was channelled into a book, *New Deal for Coal*, which he persuaded his close friend, George Weidenfeld, to publish as part of an emerging national debate about the future of this essential commodity. Coal dust ran through the veins of the Labour movement, and Wilson's book quickly became a blueprint for a nationalised industry. Whereas others argued for nationalisation from an emotional or ideological position, Wilson's was a more sober and rational justification. He advocated state ownership in the cause of greater efficiency, to allow the amalgamation of pits and the development of new coalfields, and to guarantee adequate funding for research; his book also dealt with the nuts and bolts of how nationalisation would work.

Will Lawther, the leader of the Miners' Federation of Great Britain – soon to be renamed the National Union of Mineworkers (NUM) – a significant Labour affiliate, was vociferous in his praise, describing the book as 'one of the most important statements issued on this despised and rejected industry'. Lawther was one of a growing band of influential figures who wanted to see Harold Wilson in Parliament.

But the rules of the civil service required Wilson to resign before he could even be considered as a parliamentary candidate: to abandon secure, well-paid employment without any indication as to whether he'd be given a seat to contest, let alone have any occupation after the election. He left with the customary OBE for his civil service work.

7

HAVING taken leave of absence from Oxford to join the
service, his job as a lecturer had been held open for
him under special wartime arrangements. At his lunch with
Beveridge (who was still Master of University College, despite
frequent absences), Wilson was assured that his return would
be welcome in any interregnum. He returned, temporarily.

Several Constituency Labour Parties took an interest in
the 27-year-old 'B'-list candidate. In the spring of 1944,
Wilson accepted a nomination for Peterborough but lost
at the selection meeting to a local man. He was then short-
listed for the Elland constituency of Leeds, followed in rapid
succession by Sowerby Bridge, Darlington, Grimsby and
Ormskirk. Unfortunately, none of these were Labour seats,
so even if selected there was little optimism about winning.
Nevertheless, he arranged to appear before the selection
committee at Ormskirk before travelling straight to Grimsby
to repeat the ordeal.

Ormskirk was then a mainly agricultural area of Lancashire
within the Liverpool city boundary. It stretched out to the
coast at Southport as well as inland towards Preston. Won

by a local farmer for Labour in 1929, the MP had followed MacDonald when the party split two years later, resigning in 1939 to cause a wartime by-election. The unchallenged winner had been Stephen King-Hall, a naval officer (and playwright) who stood as a National Government candidate (thus continuing his predecessor's link with MacDonald's breakaway) but switched to 'Independent' once elected.

Having impressed the selection committee and secured the Labour candidacy at Ormskirk, Wilson withdrew from the Grimsby selection and then turned down a late approach from Edmonton, a safe North London Labour seat that would have provided a guaranteed passage to the Commons. Ormskirk didn't offer anything like the same easy ride. However, good fortune came to his aid once more. Having supported King-Hall in 1939, the Conservatives felt betrayed at his conversion to Independent and decided to run a candidate against him. It would be a three-way fight, which meant a split in the anti-Labour vote.

The first general election in a decade was eventually called for July 1945. Harold was ubiquitous in Ormskirk throughout the short campaign, usually accompanied by his proud father, Herbert. His speeches by all accounts were dull and overburdened with technical detail, and he was far more impressive in the more spontaneous question-and-answer sessions. Overall, it was a good-natured contest, the only venom being confined to a group of Conservatives who abused King-Hall as a turncoat. Wilson remained on friendly terms with his opponent, who went on to establish the Hansard Society dedicated to the enhancement of parliamentary democracy, a subject close to Wilson's heart.

The fifth of July was election day. It seemed inconceivable that the Prime Minister wouldn't be rewarded for Hitler's defeat. Such was his stature as a war hero that neither Labour nor the Liberals put forward a candidate in Churchill's own constituency of Woodford.

There was a three-week gap before the votes were counted to allow time for service personnel scattered across the globe to participate. On 26 July, Harold and Herbert attended the Ormskirk count. The result was: King-Hall 11,848; Greg (the Conservative candidate) 23,104; Wilson 30,126. Ormskirk was part of the Labour landslide, one of its 239 gains that night. The party had won an outright majority for the first time.

Churchill and his Foreign Secretary Anthony Eden had flown back from Potsdam on 25 July, having paused the negotiations with our allies on how the spoils of victory would be divided. The Americans and Russians confidently expected to see the two men return. One can only imagine the bemusement of Stalin in particular when the men who flew back to the German town on 28 July were Clement Attlee and Ernest Bevin. The idea of any leader being ousted in an election would have been perplexing enough for the Russian leader, but for Churchill, an internationally revered figure, to suffer such a fate must have been incomprehensible.

The new Prime Minister and Foreign Secretary flew to Potsdam straight from a Saturday-morning meeting of the Parliamentary Labour Party (PLP) in central London, where Bevin had moved a vote of confidence in Attlee to scupper an attempt by Herbert Morrison to usurp him as leader. Harold Wilson was among the victorious Labour MPs who packed the hall and joined in the extended ovation that followed the vote in favour of the motion.

Wilson had hired a car so that he could drive north to his constituency immediately after the meeting, avoiding the trains that would be overcrowded at the start of the bank holiday weekend. Four fellow Lancashire MPs asked if he had room in the car for them, including George Tomlinson, a Bolton MP who had been a junior minister in the coalition.

Unfortunately for Harold and his travelling companions, the car blew a gasket, and, when that was fixed, the brakes failed – just as Wilson was taking his last remaining passenger, Tomlinson, to his front door.

On 2 August, the member for Ormskirk attended the chamber of the House of Commons for the first time to be sworn in as a Member of Parliament. This ceremony requires MPs to queue at the government despatch box to take the oath of allegiance followed by a handshake with the Speaker. One of the Labour whips approached Harold to say Manny Shinwell, the Minister of Fuel and Power, wanted him to be his Parliamentary Private Secretary (PPS).

It is unusual for a new MP to be given any kind of government role, even as a PPS, a position which isn't really on the ministerial ladder, despite often being described as its lowest rung. It carries no salary and no responsibilities other than to be the 'eyes and ears' of the minister in the House while they pursue their ministerial responsibilities elsewhere in Whitehall. In the 1945 Parliament, however, novices were in demand. The Labour government was desperately short of ministerial experience given that two-thirds of their 393 MPs were newly elected.

Although extremely young, Wilson, with his brilliant academic achievements, recognised ability as a civil servant and particular expertise on all aspects of the coal industry, must have been an attractive prospect for Shinwell. Unlike ministerial appointments, which are the exclusive gift of the Prime Minister, the choice of a PPS could be made by a Cabinet minister. Wilson accepted the offer, only for a better one to emerge a few days later.

Returning from Potsdam to the more prosaic work of finalising the junior ranks of his government, Attlee asked the No. 10 switchboard to track down the MP for Ormskirk. Wilson had returned to University College, Oxford (incidentally, Attlee's alma mater), after being sworn in, to do some lecturing while waiting for the King's Speech that would herald the commencement of the new parliament.

Coming back to the college from the shops on a Saturday morning, Wilson was told that 10 Downing Street had been trying to contact him. He returned the call and was put through to the Prime Minister. Attlee, a man renowned for never using six words where one would do, offered the young, newly elected MP a job in government, as Parliamentary Undersecretary of State to George Tomlinson, Wilson's unfortunate passenger on the recent fateful car journey to Lancashire. Tomlinson now headed up the Ministry of Works. 'Said you tried to kill him,' Attlee concluded in his clipped tones, 'but doesn't hold it against you.'

This really was the first of the three rungs on the ministerial ladder (the other two being Minister of State and, at the top, Secretary of State). A couple of other newly elected MPs went straight into government, but both were much older than the member for Ormskirk, who was the youngest office holder in the entire government. Almost every MP begins his or her career in Parliament as a backbencher (rather than on the front benches, where ministers and shadow ministers sit). Harold Wilson, a minister before the 1945 parliament had even convened, wouldn't occupy those benches until the 1950s, and then only briefly.

His meteoric rise was disadvantageous in one respect. The value of starting on the back benches is that new MPs generally have time to get their bearings, understand how Parliament works, the rules of debate, and, perhaps more pertinently in Wilson's case, how to deliver an effective speech in the very unusual (and confrontational) setting of the Commons chamber. The deliberations of the House of Commons weren't allowed to be broadcast on radio until 1978 (and weren't televised until 11 years after that). For a new MP in the 1940s it would therefore have been even more important to absorb the gladiatorial atmosphere by participating on whatever subject took their fancy. As a minister, Wilson could only participate when scheduled and as a representative of the government.

Far from being able to ease himself in, Wilson had immediately to assume the heavy responsibilities of a government minister. The maiden speech an MP makes in the House is a personal landmark steeped in tradition. Delivered from the back benches, it is supposed to praise the MP's immediate predecessor and draw attention to the delights of his or her constituency. By custom it is heard in silence, with no interventions allowed.

But Harold Wilson had to make his maiden speech from the despatch box where ministers speak. He was unable to mention King-Hall or dwell on the attractions of Ormskirk because he spoke as a representative of the Ministry of Works, and on a serious and contentious issue. The Houses of Parliament had been damaged in air raids on 14 separate occasions during the war. Repairs to MPs' office accommodation was well behind schedule. The Ministry's newest minister had to defend his department against a raucously critical House. He certainly wasn't heard in silence and there were interventions galore. It was a baptism of fire from which Wilson emerged badly singed.

8

H E had much more success at the ministry itself. A serious backlog had built up in the provision of the shells for prefabricated homes. A third of Britain's houses had been damaged or destroyed in the war. While the Ministry of Health formulated housing policy, responsibility for construction rested with the Ministry of Works. Health decided how many houses were to be built and Works got on with building them. The department's Permanent Secretary, Sir Percival Robinson, was every bit as old-school civil service as his name suggests, and he was soon raising Wilson's hackles. After being questioned by the new junior minister on the backlog, Sir Percival made the mistake of disappearing on a three-week summer holiday, compounding this error by complaining about Wilson convening a meeting in his absence that had included some lower-grade officials. Protocol in the class-ridden civil service demanded that only its senior ranks be allowed to mix with government ministers. Sir Percival had sealed his fate. Within weeks he'd been moved out of Whitehall and into exile (on the Suez Canal Company).

This incident demonstrated not just the youthful minister's ruthless streak but also his standing with senior Cabinet colleagues. Wilson had now worked with two of the most notable of them, albeit at one remove. His work at Trade in the war had been closely aligned with the Ministry of Labour and its imperious Secretary of State, Ernest Bevin, and at the Ministry of Works he'd come to the attention of the Health Secretary, Nye Bevan, whose remit also covered housing. The two men with similar-sounding surnames were on opposite wings of the Labour Party. Bevin, by now Foreign Secretary, was the scourge of the left while Bevan was its leading figure in the PLP. It is said that, on a rail journey with colleagues, a Labour figure happened to remark that Nye Bevan was his own worst enemy. 'Not while I'm alive he ain't,' Bevin is said to have interjected in his soft Somerset accent.

Nye Bevan was to become a defining influence, as we shall see. In 1945, while seeking to overcome the fervent opposition of the Conservatives and the medical profession to the creation of the NHS, the mercurial Welshman was also determined to ensure that the house-building programme remain on course. He couldn't fail to be impressed by the way the new junior minister set about solving the central cause of the backlog, which was a shortage of timber. Wilson had wanted to source additional supplies from North America, but was told by Board of Trade officials that his only option was Canada because there were no softwoods available for export in the United States despite timber being far more plentiful there. By chance Wilson was given the opportunity to travel to the States when the Prime Minister appointed him to lead a British delegation to a United Nations conference on food distribution. The mission involved three weeks of long and tedious meetings but there were more agreeable aspects. Mary came out to join him with infant Robin for a few days and there was an unexpected development in the quest for timber. Visiting Washington at the same time was Tom Meyer, who'd recently succeeded his father as head of Montague L. Meyer Ltd, Britain's biggest timber merchant. He and Wilson were of a similar age and quickly became firm friends. Tom told Harold that, contrary to the Board of Trade advice, there was timber available for export in the United States for those who knew where to look.

A Ministry of Works purchasing team had just gone to Canada, and Wilson asked that they stop over in Washington on their way back. He contrived a meeting between the civil service team and Tom Meyer, and as a result more timber was acquired, from the United States as well as from Canada.

Upon his return from America, Wilson was required to report to Parliament on the UN conference, which had produced a formula to create price stability internationally in order to avoid the food shortages in poorer countries that had followed in the wake of the First World War. In this debate Wilson's mastery of detail impressed the House more than his oratory. One political correspondent summed up his speaking style thus: 'Technically, Mr Wilson is a terrible speaker – he gabbles his words half the time as if he himself were bored of them. He builds cliché on statistic on cliché in mountainous sandwiches of tedium; he has no gestures to speak of and very little variety of inflection.'

It was a cruel but fair assessment. At this early stage of his political career Wilson was more technocrat than states-man. He certainly knew how Whitehall worked, but he was a parliamentary novice. Nevertheless, his success with timber and at the UN led to another rapid promotion, to Secretary for Overseas Trade, a junior-ministerial position. Within two years of being elected to Parliament, and at the tender age (for a politician) of 31, he was now one rung off the top of the ministerial ladder.

This new position placed him in direct contact with two of the most influential political figures in his life. The first was Sir Stafford Cripps, yet to assume the office for which he is still best remembered – Chancellor of the Exchequer. At this stage Cripps was President of the Board of Trade (or Business Secretary, as the post is known today) and Wilson's new boss. For a long time, Cripps had been his political hero, the man Harold most admired and wanted to emulate among a galaxy of stars in the 1945 Labour government. This may have been because Cripps shared Wilson's Christian socialism as well as having an unrelenting sense of public duty. Cripps had been one of the few Labour MPs to survive the National Government landslide of 1931, but eight years later he'd been expelled (along with Nye Bevan) for advocating with others on the left – most controversially, the Communist Party of Great Britain (CPGB) – a 'Popular Front' against fascism. Bevan sought and achieved a speedy reconciliation with Labour, but Cripps refused to renounce his opinion and continued to sit as an Independent MP throughout the war. Incredibly, this did not prevent him being appointed by Churchill to be our ambassador to Moscow, or from serving in the coalition government, most importantly as Minister for Aircraft Production. He hadn't returned to the Labour fold until 1945, in time to stand as the party's candidate again in his Bristol seat.

The second influential figure that the promotion brought Wilson into contact with was Barbara Castle. As a Minister of State, he was now entitled to appoint a PPS. He chose the 37-year-old MP for Blackburn. Like Wilson, Castle (née Betts) had been to Oxford, albeit five years in advance of him. She'd been elected to Parliament in the same 1945 landslide as one of only 24 women MPs (21 of them on Labour's benches). This was perhaps less surprising in the context of women only having been granted the same voting rights as men 17 years previously. Castle had already served as PPS to Stafford Cripps, and it's highly likely that it was Cripps who recommended her to Wilson. Barbara Castle would remain an ally for the rest of his political life.

In his new role the already much-travelled minister would spend even more time abroad. Despatched immediately to an international trade conference on tariffs in Geneva, Wilson was then asked by Attlee to support the increasingly unwell Foreign Secretary Ernest Bevin in the difficult and complex negotiations on trade he was having with Russia. As soon as Wilson arrived in Moscow, Bevin was sent home on doctors' orders following a mild heart attack. The young, newly promoted Minister of State was placed in charge of the entire UK delegation. His adversary was the shrewd, experienced Anastas Mikoyan. Twenty-one years Wilson's senior, the Armenian was the only significant Bolshevik survivor from the latter days of Lenin. He would continue to serve through the Stalin and Khrushchev eras and eventually retire quietly as number two to Brezhnev in 1965. As Russia's Minister of Trade in these negotiations his mouth must have watered at the delicacy placed before him in the shape of the novice UK minister. It was during these negotiations that Wilson, a smoker of cigarettes for many years, began to smoke a pipe. He said it was to enhance his negotiating technique – that the paraphernalia associated with filling a pipe, as well as lighting and relighting the thing, provided props to aid the thought process. But with the moustache he had grown and the waistcoats he invariably wore, it may also have been an attempt to make him appear older than his years.

The Armenian and the Yorkshireman certainly had much to resolve. Given that there hadn't been any meaningful trading arrangements since the revolution of 1917, they were beginning the process of establishing an Anglo-Soviet trade deal from scratch. Wilson soon found that vodka played an important role in lubricating the negotiations. During one epic 16-course banquet, with each one necessitating a speech and a toast, the Russians learnt two things about the tenderfoot leading the UK delegation. The first was that he was no pushover; the second was that he could hold his drink.

Wilson's remit was to import what Britain needed (principally wheat and, once again, timber) as cheaply as possible while maximising export opportunities, which Cripps considered to be 'a matter of life and death' for Britain. As for the Russian remit, Mikoyan needed to alleviate the substantial debt obligations built up during the war and improve his country's access to machinery and advanced aerospace technology. In respect of the latter, the USSR wanted 20

Rolls-Royce jet engines. This Russian demand was already under consideration when Wilson joined the talks, yet they would become a stick to beat him with years later when it was alleged by some press observers that he was pro-Russian and even a Communist sympathiser.

Ernie Bevin, as Foreign Secretary, was deeply sceptical about including engines in any trade agreement. The Americans had also made the UK government aware of its concerns. While Russia had been an ally in the Second World War, the 'Iron Curtain' (as Churchill described it) was falling across Eastern Europe and the security service was wary about giving Russia access to our technological know-how. Stafford Cripps was already viewed with suspicion by the United States, who feared that, as our ambassador in Moscow, he may have gone native.

As mentioned, the Rolls-Royce engines were already on the negotiating table when Wilson arrived. Furthermore, because of his junior position and the sensitivity of the issue it is inconceivable that he, as stand-in UK delegation leader, would have made any concessions on this element without checking with Bevin and Cripps first. In the end, no Anglo-Soviet trade agreement could be reached, but this episode was important, not just because of the mistaken notion that Wilson was sympathetic to Communism, but also as a factor in fuelling the paranoia that he was to develop about the security service. MI5 had already opened a file on James Harold Wilson, kept under the pseudonym 'Norman John Worthington'. In respect of these trade negotiations, the file noted (presumably to its subject's credit) that the Communist newspaper in Britain, the *Daily Worker*, had castigated Wilson for having 'inexcusably failed to conclude a trading agreement with the Soviet Union'.

On the return flight from Moscow, the pilot overshot the runway, leaving Wilson with a cracked rib as the only memento of the Anglo-Russian trade deal. When the usually austere Stafford Cripps heard about the accident, he demonstrated a rare flash of humour, lamenting 'the things some ministers will do to get publicity'.

9

THE Moscow trip did attract publicity, albeit for the crash landing as much as the negotiations. Even though the talks failed, the new minister emerged with credit. The deal had broken down on finance rather than trade and a senior figure at the Moscow embassy reported that Wilson had 'conducted the talks with great skill and firmness and proved himself fully a match for the redoubtable and much more experienced negotiator Mikoyan'.

Being away so much and for so long may have brought him to prominence in his career but it also had its drawbacks. Mary had hardly seen her husband. Living mainly in college rooms at Oxford with Robin, who was now old enough to notice his father's absence, she also spent time at the wartime Richmond flat, which her parents now occupied, and with Harold's parents in Cornwall. She had no home to call her own and, for long periods, a husband in name only. Professionally, while Wilson had made his mark as a minister, he'd impressed the civil service more than his fellow MPs. As for Ormskirk, even at a time when an MP wasn't expected to spend much time in their constituency, his absence had been noticed by the local Labour Party, to which he'd made a rash and unfulfilled promise of monthly visits. But if these were problems, they were the problems of success rather than failure. And that success was about to intensify.

Clem Attlee was plagued by leadership challenges. Morrison had already attempted regicide from the right of the party. Now, in 1947, Stafford Cripps was campaigning from the left for a 'stronger' replacement (which meant either Ernest Bevin or himself). When told about this by Cripps, who'd decided to stab his leader in the front rather than the back, Attlee reacted with typical equanimity. Having first ascertained that his old ally Bevin was as supportive as ever, he dealt with Cripps by promoting him. A new government department was created specifically to meet his detractor's main criticism, which was a lack of integrated planning. Cripps became Minister of Economic Affairs, and the challenge was averted, but there was now a vacancy at the Board of Trade. There was wide consensus about who should fill it. Wilson had managed to make an impression on each of what were known as Labour's 'Big Five' – Attlee, Bevin, Morrison, Cripps and Dalton.

On 29 September 1947, Wilson was appointed President of the Board of Trade. At 31 years and seven months, he was the youngest Cabinet minister since Lord Henry Petty in 1806. The extraordinary speed of Wilson's elevation was even more remarkable given its lack of connection with any part of the Labour movement. Attlee had sacrificed a legal career to pursue philanthropic work in London's East End; Bevin was a trade unionist, creator of the mighty Transport and General Workers' Union (TGWU); Morrison was steeped in municipal government, having risen through the London County Council; Cripps was a leading socialist intellectual and Hugh Dalton's politics had been forged in student activism.

Wilson had hardly even attended a party meeting. He did not have Nye Bevan's emotional attachment to Labour, but neither did he have Hugh Gaitskell's condescension towards it (brilliantly described by Malcolm Muggeridge as 'like a High Church clergyman with a slum parish'). Wilson may have carried his political convictions lightly but that is not to say he didn't have any. His approach to the Labour Party was like his approach to religion – a believer but never devout. A man of considerable intellect but not an intellectual, a pragmatist rather than an idealist. And he wasn't one to wear his heart on his sleeve, having been taught by Herbert and Ethel never to display emotion. His parents' influence was clear in other ways. Their son was a perpetual boy scout, always trying to do his best and keen to display the badges he'd acquired. An irrepressible show-off, delighting in his own cleverness but in a benign way, with neither malice nor arrogance.

Observing him in action as a Cabinet minister, prominent businessman Sir Raymond Streat said of the newly appointed Trade minister: 'He is quick on the uptake – too well versed in economics and civil service work to rant or rave like a soap-box socialist... he lets his mind work on lines that come naturally to a young economist with civil service experience. We shall get on easily with him.'

Another pen portrait came from Honor Balfour in the *Birmingham Gazette*:

A nice, quiet, plump, good-humoured fellow who had not yet quite got used to being the person of importance that he now is. In repose his manner, his greying temple and his formal clothes give him an appearance of middle age. But once he begins to speak, he cannot restrain his liveliness nor his interest in a subject or a person.

Nothing Wilson did during his three years and seven months as a member of Attlee's Cabinet was to match the drama of his eventual departure, but there were some notable developments in between.

On the domestic front, the couple's need for proper accommodation had been accelerated by Harold's promotion and Mary's second pregnancy. The Cabinet post meant there would be no time even for the occasional lecture at Oxford and a consequential loss of college accommodation. On 7 May 1948 Mary gave birth to another son, Giles (godparents Mr and Mrs Attlee). By then the Wilsons had acquired a home of their own.

As the name suggests, Hampstead Garden Suburb is in that salubrious district of north-west London famous for its heath and the bohemian reputation of its residents. Promotion to the Cabinet increased Harold's salary fivefold, which meant he could now afford the three-bedroom house with a substantial garden and a nursery for four-year-old Robin nearby. It had cost the equivalent of a year's salary, but the family of four was now complete and properly housed in a single location.

The new job was naturally more demanding. Harold was quickly off to Moscow again, this time to negotiate a trade deal without the added complication of finance or aircraft engines. Basically, the talks centred on timber, a beam of which seemed to run through Wilson's early career. Britain needed the stuff and Russia was desperate for the machinery to cut it with.

Mikoyan, still heading up the Russian delegation, was delighted to cross swords with his old adversary again, and this time, in three days of intensive negotiation, an agreement was reached. Keen to celebrate it and show how influential he was, Mikoyan arranged for Wilson to dine with Stalin at the Kremlin. Wilson declined because he was due in London to attend a dinner at 10 Downing Street that same evening in honour of King George VI. What MI5 would have made of the new Cabinet minister, given their suspicions of Communist leanings, pulling out of dinner with his own head of state to break bread with that of Russia can only be imagined.

It would have undoubtedly led to negative press coverage, but Wilson's first experience of this was to come soon enough. In the summer of 1948, he answered questions in the House about the shortage of children's shoes, which were still being rationed. The President of the Board of Trade told the Commons that the main reason for the shortage was increased demand due to the post-war baby boom. That same evening, in a speech to an audience of industrialists in Birmingham, he elaborated, saying that another aspect of the problem was that parents were now more prosperous and rightly demanded better-quality footwear for their children. He contrasted this to the situation when he was a child in the 1920s, when 'half the children in my class never had boots or shoes to their feet. They wore clogs because they lasted longer than shoes of a comparable price. I have been up there again. The children of my old school are now running about with decent pairs of shoes because their fathers are in safe jobs and have got the social security which we promised our people.'

An unremarkable speech by a government minister doing what ministers tend to do, extol the virtues of their government. But it was reported very differently. The reference to clogs was ignored and an inference made that Wilson had been among the 'half the children' in his class who 'never had boots or shoes to their feet'. Wilson, it was reported, had claimed to be so poor that he'd been sent to school in bare feet. He'd claimed no such thing, but the Labour mayor of Huddersfield then made things worse. He was a teacher at the school in question (albeit not when Wilson was a pupil), and told the press that the President of the Board of Trade had 'overstepped the mark'. With more experience he would have just let it all die down, but instead the outraged minister issued a public denial, pointing out that while he had never gone to school barefooted 'before the war', many children had. This was promptly reported as 'during the war' – cue an even greater press barrage against him. The 'barefoot boy' episode would be quoted against Wilson for the next 25 years with only his biographers bothering to set the record straight.

Rationing for children's shoes didn't end until May 1949, and for adults' shoes three months later. Despite its unpopularity with the public, many in the Labour Party considered rationing to be a vital mechanism for a fairer society. Others argued that it dampened demand and reduced the country's dependency on imported goods. Wilson didn't agree. He arranged a bonfire of rationing regulations in his time at the Board of Trade, even contriving a photo opportunity tearing up a ration book to illustrate his point. When civil servants advised him to use rationing to discourage Dior's iconic 'New Look' because of the abundance of material it required, Wilson made the reasonable point that government 'can't dictate what length women shall wear their skirts'.

By 1949 his predecessor at the Board of Trade, Stafford Cripps, by now Chancellor of the Exchequer, had become convinced that sterling needed to be devalued. Wilson had come to the same conclusion. On a trade visit to Canada, he'd seen that, at over four dollars to the pound, our currency was drastically out of line with economic trends. British goods were too expensive to buy abroad, while cheap imported goods from America distorted our balance of payments to the extent that Britain spent £750 million more abroad than it received. Exports by British manufacturers had fallen by 60 per cent. Many other trading nations were faced with the same dilemma, but if Britain devalued it would have global ramifications. Well over a quarter of the world's commerce was conducted in sterling, and 19 non-sterling countries had their national currency pegged to the value of the pound.

When Cripps was taken ill, Wilson was effectively placed in ministerial charge of the Treasury, along with Gaitskell and another young minister, Douglas Jay. It became Wilson's responsibility to authorise the sale of gold reserves, which, in the absence of devaluation, was necessary to try to balance the books. It was a role that Wilson described as 'like watching yourself bleed to death'.

In September, with Cripps back from sick leave, the decision was taken. Sterling's value was reduced from $4.03 to the pound to $2.80. In the modern world of floating currencies, it's hard to appreciate what an enormous issue devaluation was: so momentous it warranted a BBC broadcast to the nation by Sir Stafford Cripps on the evening of 18 September 1949. He pitched devaluation as an alternative to high unemployment and cuts to social services. Wilson would have cause to remember the concluding sentence of that broadcast. 'This is a step,' Cripps said, 'that we cannot and shall not repeat.'

10

DEVALUING the pound five months before a general election was hardly ideal. It may not have been solely responsible for Labour's poor showing at the 1950 election, but it didn't help. The unavoidable privations of a post-war period when Britain's debt was more than 200 per cent of the country's total wealth (GDP) was a more obvious explanation. Churchill, still the great war hero lauded across the world, remained at the helm of a Conservative Party now more in tune with the zeitgeist than it had been in 1945. The National Health Service they'd once opposed was now acclaimed, and no commitments were made to reverse the nationalisation of rail and coal. By and large, they supported the welfare state, full employment and a mixed economy. Their reward was an extraordinary revival. Labour's 186-seat majority should have heralded a decade in office, and the party did win the 1950 general election – but only just: by six seats.

Boundary changes had put a significant chunk of Ormskirk into a new constituency closer to Liverpool called Huyton. Harold Wilson won the seat, but, despite its composition being more favourable to Labour, his majority was a slim 834. The economic situation that necessitated devaluation had generated measures unpopular with Labour voters. The number of new homes was revised down by 25,000 and a shilling (5p) charge for prescriptions introduced to try to contain the spiralling cost of the NHS. Medicine provided free at the point of need had been an important feature of Attlee's 'New Jerusalem'. Nye Bevan, the Health Secretary, had argued against prescription charges in Cabinet, as did Wilson, but neither man resigned when the argument was lost.

After the election Bevan was moved from Health to be Minister of Labour, while Wilson was reappointed President of the Board of Trade. The two men had become friends as well as allies. Nye Bevan had recognised the younger man's capabilities ever since the prefab backlog had been resolved and urged Attlee to appoint Wilson as the only realistic choice when the post of President of the Board of Trade became vacant. He'd even canvassed his ally's name as a possible leadership candidate in one of his frequent outbursts of dissatisfaction with Attlee, a suggestion that Wilson considered preposterous, and others cited as an example of Bevan's poor judgement.

Wilson admired Bevan but considered many of the 'Bevanites', as Bevan's three dozen or so devoted followers in Parliament were known, to be self-indulgent (although Barbara Castle, a prominent Bevanite, was excused from this criticism). He particularly deplored the extremism of some of Nye Bevan's followers in the constituency parties. Bevan and Wilson shared a fundamental belief in democratic socialism, as opposed to the revolutionary variety that many of Bevan's followers flirted with.

Prescription charges had been a bitter pill for Bevan to swallow (to use an appropriate metaphor), but he and Wilson had accepted the economic imperative. In respect of the NHS, both men's position was 'thus far and no further'. Hugh Gaitskell, Wilson's admirer during the war, when he'd counselled against losing him from the civil service, had become Chancellor after ill health forced Sir Stafford Cripps to step down. Gaitskell and Bevan were sworn adversaries, with Gaitskell exerting as powerful (if less charismatic) an influence on the right of the party as Bevan did on the left.

Bevan's theory that the cost of the NHS would reduce as the health of the nation improved already looked naive. Pent-up demand had been underestimated, particularly in respect of dental treatment and ophthalmology. Lack of oral hygiene and a poor diet meant that few working-class adults were free of tooth decay. Rather than go through years of pain, a grateful public besieged the NHS to have what teeth they still had removed and replaced by a full set of dentures. At the same time, queues formed outside opticians to acquire rudimentary, wire-framed NHS spectacles. Gaitskell decided to raise some revenue by charging for teeth and glasses as part of his first Budget.

The new Chancellor wasn't just grappling with the rising costs of healthcare; he was also required to increase Britain's defence budget, mainly because of the Korean War. When Gaitskell's NHS charges were discussed in Cabinet, Bevan was furious and ultimately implacable. At a speech to party activists in east London a few days before the Budget he upped the ante by stating that he wouldn't remain part of a government that introduced any further health charges. Labour's fragile majority meant that even a small rebellion could lead to a government defeat, and Sam Watson, secretary of the powerful Durham Miners' Association and Bevan's old ally, spoke for many when he said: 'The trade union movement has a traditional dislike of resignations when members cannot get their own way and a greater dislike when, following full opportunity for discussion, a majority decision is cast aside.'

Nye Bevan's reaction to NHS charges was predictable; Harold Wilson's was a surprise. He had supported Bevan's arguments in Cabinet but from a different perspective. Wilson's stance wasn't so much about teeth and glasses, although he accepted that such charges would undermine the founding principles of the NHS. However, that principle had already been breached by charging for prescriptions and was no longer inviolate. His stance was less emotional and more pragmatic. NHS charges were being imposed to finance an armaments programme that Britain didn't have the capacity to meet. He knew from his experience at Works and Trade that the necessary raw materials simply weren't available in the quantities needed. One reason for this was stockpiling by America, the major protagonist in a Korean War that was requiring Britain to increase its defence budget. Parliament was being asked to authorise NHS charges to raise money that could never be spent.

Efforts to avoid Cabinet resignations weren't helped by the three most influential Labour figures all being in poor health. Cripps, who had influence over both Bevan and Gaitskell, had only another year to live; Ernie Bevin, who, as Lord Privy Seal, tried to broker a deal between the two men, died in harness a few weeks later (the key to his red box still clasped in his powerful fist); and Attlee, the captain at the helm, had been hospitalised with a duodenal ulcer. The Prime Minister knew that if he forced Gaitskell to compromise, his Chancellor would resign rather than his Minister of Labour. The dilemma probably didn't help his stress-related condition. Bevan, understanding the damage his resignation would do, tried hard to convince Wilson not to resign with him. However, as his ally calmly pointed out, Bevan was the significant figure whose departure would do 98 per cent of the damage. Wilson and junior minister John Freeman (the other potential departee) would only represent the remaining 2 per cent.

Nye Bevan's 'personal statement', as resignation speeches are described in the Commons, was made on 23 April 1951. It wasn't a success. Even his biographer and devoted friend Michael Foot admitted that 'no single cheer greeted his peroration', which was full of bombast and personal attacks on the Chancellor. Resignation speeches are not a requirement, but Wilson felt that, as Bevan had taken the opportunity, he must as well. His personal statement was made the following day. After six years in Parliament, it was his first speech from the back benches. The distinction is greater than simply indicating where a speaker is situated in the chamber. Ministers contributing from the despatch box at least have somewhere to place their notes as well as a substantial prop to stand behind. The despatch box gives an important rhetorical advantage. A backbencher must stand, notes in hand, like a chorister in a church pew.

Mary was in the gallery, watching her husband as he rose to deliver a very different speech from Bevan's the previous day. It was well ordered, unsentimental and free of any rancour or personal attacks. The *Manchester Guardian* described it as 'a lesson in how to resign'. In a colourful comparison of the two speeches, one commentator observed that Mr Bevan 'had ended with his boats ablaze. Mr Wilson's boats carried fire-fighting equipment.'

Many of those following Wilson's career say that this marked the end of Harold the technocrat and the birth of Harold the politician.

11

D ID Wilson resign out of self-interest? It seems unlikely given that he could well have been consigning himself to the political wilderness. In any case, it attracted little media attention. As Wilson had predicted, all the publicity centred on Bevan. On a personal level, it reduced his salary by four-fifths, from a Cabinet minister's £5,000 a year to an MP's £1,000.

It was certainly un-Wilson-like. Nye was the impulsive one, not Harold.

Hugh Dalton labelled Wilson 'Nye's little dog' and it stuck. Whether he liked it or not, the resignation made Wilson a leading Bevanite.

The self-interest calculation could have been that Bevan would become leader after Attlee. But Wilson knew that his friend didn't have wide enough support among MPs to succeed. Wilson's belief was that Gaitskell was the man whose actions had been dictated by ambition; that he'd refused to compromise on a defence budget that he knew was unrealisable precisely because it would require a corresponding reduction in health spending, force Bevan's resignation and boost his own chances of succeeding Attlee.

Of course, what Wilson couldn't know was that Labour would soon be out of office. Five months after the resignations, Clem Attlee called a snap election for 25 October 1951. A stronger economy and the relaxation of wartime regulations convinced him that Labour's prospects were good. Another factor was that King George VI was due to tour the Commonwealth early in 1952 and had told Attlee that he may need to cancel for fear of his government with its slim majority being toppled in his absence.

It was a significant general election, one in which the distortions of our electoral system led to Labour, with a quarter of a million more votes than the Conservatives, conceding power to a Tory majority of 17 seats. For Harold Wilson at least, there was an advantage in this setback. His constituency party had strongly supported his decision to resign, and he'd used the spare time that resignation gave him to visit Huyton more often than he'd ever visited Ormskirk. He'd even introduced a weekly constituency surgery, which was a rarity back then. The hard work paid off: his majority increased to 1,193. He'd also fallen on his feet financially. Tom Meyer, the man he'd befriended in America on his quest for timber, offered him a part-time job at Montague L. Meyer. As well as a salary of £1,500 a year, he would have an office at their HQ on the Strand, a paid secretary and a car. Given that there was little office space in Parliament and no secretarial allowance, these were valuable perks.

Wilson probably knew about this job offer before he resigned, just as he'd have calculated that displaying an independent streak would boost his standing in the constituency, so the decision to resign may have taken these factors into account, but they didn't dictate it.

Mary Wilson recalled this as the only period in their long marriage when her husband had sleepless nights, pacing the floor thinking through the consequences of resignation. If he knew about the job offer from Tom Meyer, he could not have known there'd be an election within six months. He genuinely believed that Gaitskell's Budget decisions were wrong and that by adding his threat of resignation to Bevan's he may have forced Attlee to overrule them. The charge of devious-ness doesn't stick. It is easy to pillory pragmatism as lack of principle, but it's equally easy to conclude that principle was behind Wilson's resignation, and what is beyond doubt is that Wilson was right: the enhanced defence budget would prove impossible to spend. The new Conservative administration swiftly reduced projected spending on armaments. Prime Minister Churchill told the Commons on 5 December 1951: 'It appears by accident perhaps, not for the best of motives, that the Right Honourable Member for Ebbw Vale [Bevan, and by extension Wilson] happened to be right.'

NHS charges had been imposed to pay for an armaments programme that never materialised.

The Labour Party moved further to the left after losing office. The beauty contests that personified these shifts were the elections for the seven-seat constituency section of Labour's National Executive Committee (NEC), voted on exclusively by local activists, and the shadow cabinet elections that were the preserve of Labour MPs. (When in government, then as now, Cabinet appointments were in the gift of the party leader; in opposition, then but not now, shadow cabinet members were elected by the PLP.)

At a bad-tempered 1952 Labour conference in Morecambe, the constituency section was dominated by Bevanites, with the man himself topping the poll and Wilson ousting Hugh Dalton, who was said to have had his ankles nipped by 'Nye's little dog'. Clem Attlee remained unchallenged as leader – a situation hardly imaginable today, when defeated leaders usually resign within hours of the contest. The Bevanites did less well in the shadow cabinet elections, although none of their leading lights were standing. Bevan was busy trying to oust Herbert Morrison as deputy leader, where again the electorate was Labour MPs. He failed, as he would again the following year.

By resigning with Bevan, Wilson had to live with the consequences, both positive and negative. On policy issues Wilson demonstrated his Bevanite credentials in his support for steel nationalisation. There was no posturing in this. It was an issue Wilson believed in (as he was to prove in government when he created the British Steel Corporation).

But while support for Bevan had boosted his popularity among the rank and file it had damaged his position among Labour colleagues in Parliament. He was ambitious enough to realise that advancement depended on their support and was keen to assert his independence, describing himself as a co-belligerent of Bevan rather than a satellite. More importantly, he avoided any animosity with Bevan's bête noire, Hugh Gaitskell. While not remotely interested in attending the gatherings Gaitskell presided over at his grand house in Frognal Gardens, Hampstead, Wilson went out of his way to forge a constructive relationship with his fellow Oxford economist. He believed that when Attlee eventually stepped down it was far more likely that Gaitskell would replace him than that Bevan would, given the latter's intemperate personality and the more moderate instincts of the majority of Labour MPs. When that happened, Wilson was determined to be Gaitskell's Chancellor. Ambition is surely not a negative trait in any profession, least of all in politics, where it's in the country's interests for men and women of ability to want to occupy high office.

The member for Huyton must have discovered backbench life in much the same way as Amazon explorers discover the lifestyle of a previously little-known tribe. He had never been active in the Labour Party and knew little of its customs or rituals. His voyage of discovery came courtesy of *Tribune*, the socialist newspaper. Founded by Cripps and written for by Orwell, it had become an organ of the Bevanites, and had developed the idea of mimicking a famous radio programme on which a group of experts would debate the major issues of the day. *Tribune* would take this *Brains Trust* format out to constituency-party gatherings with four Bevanite panellists. More often than not, Harold Wilson was one of them. It was his first real experience of the cut and thrust of political debate in town halls and community centres – and he thrived on it. When he was first consigned to the back benches, his speeches were still too long, overloaded with facts and empty of humour or rhetorical flourishes – still the 'mountainous sandwiches of tedium' that his early critic described.

Bevan advised him to 'cut out the boring detail', and touring with the *Tribune* 'brains trust' taught Wilson that

public speaking and repartee with an audience could be
enjoyable, even fun. His style became more relaxed; he
lost the affectation of clipped tones that made him sound
like an Attlee impersonator in his early radio interviews.
Huddersfield reasserted itself over Oxford and Wilson
became a formidable debater. It wasn't a persona he was
adopting so much as one he was discarding, to be more
like himself.

As for his concern that he was too closely associated
with one faction of the party, that resolved itself in 1954
when Bevan went a resignation too far. The election the
previous December had placed Nye in the shadow cabinet
with the ninth-highest vote. Wilson was thirteenth, which
in a team of 12 made him first reserve. Five months later,
Bevan resigned over what he considered to be an inadequate
frontbench response to the government's support for an
American proposal that a NATO-style collective defence
mechanism be applied in South East Asia. There'd been an
unsavoury commotion on Labour's front bench when Bevan
appeared to push Attlee out of the way in his enthusiasm to
get to the despatch box, where he duly undermined what his
leader had just said.

This incident, together with Bevan's second resignation in
three years, didn't go down well on Labour's benches. The
issue itself wasn't one that the Bevanites felt particularly
strongly about, so there was little sympathy for Bevan's
bumptiousness from friend or foe. With exquisite irony it was
Wilson who was due to take his mentor's place in the shadow
cabinet. In contrast to 1951, when Bevan urged Wilson not
to follow his example, he now expected his protégé to refuse

the position, stating that, if he did not, 'it would be the end of his political career.'

Wilson's preference was to stand in an election of Labour MPs for the vacancy Bevan had created, but the rules were clear: it had to be offered to the next-highest candidate at the previous election. His only options were to accept or refuse (in which case it would be offered to the next in line). He accepted, and his association with the Bevanites ended. It did him no harm. Even fellow Bevanites such as Richard Crossman and Barbara Castle felt that it was asking too much of Wilson to expect him to follow Bevan into the wilderness, on an issue that Bevan hadn't consulted his colleagues about and that wasn't high on anyone's list of priorities.

In the constituency section that year Wilson topped the poll. Bevan lost a challenge to Gaitskell for the position of party treasurer, and so was in neither the shadow cabinet nor the NEC. Wilson was a member of both. He was free of the Bevanite label, if not from the accusation that he was a callous opportunist ruthlessly pursuing the only cause he really cared about – himself.

He was back on the front bench but had hardly been idle during his period away. Wilson had probably travelled more than most Cabinet ministers. Montague Meyer's timber-exporting business gave the company a considerable role in East–West trade. He'd already been to the States on their behalf when, early in 1953, Wilson became the first senior Labour figure to visit the USSR since the death of Stalin. The trip, during which he'd met his old friend Mikoyan, by now deputy Prime Minister, caused a collective raised eyebrow in the press and, in all probability, the security service. However,

Wilson had taken the precaution of informing the Prime Minister of his visit personally. Churchill not only urged him to go, but notified the embassy, even offering some sage advice about what Wilson should look out for.

While in Russia, Wilson met Molotov, then the Minister of Foreign Affairs, convincing him to join what he termed the 'war on want', invoking one of Beveridge's 'five giants' to describe an international effort to fight poverty in the same way as the Allies had combined to fight Hitler. Consequently, the USSR contributed finance and technical expertise. Wilson followed this up with a book, *The War on World Poverty*, published by Victor Gollancz (founder of the Left Book Club), which advocated an International Development Authority to which developed nations would contribute an agreed proportion of national income. While Wilson always credited Gollancz with the creation of the charity War on Want, it's clear that he himself played a crucial role. As Prime Minister he would introduce a Ministry of Overseas Development and appoint a Cabinet minister as its Secretary of State.

12

WINSTON Churchill finally stepped aside for his long-time heir apparent, Sir Anthony Eden, in April 1955. Eden promptly called an election. Clem Attlee, Churchill's deputy in the wartime coalition, entered his twentieth year as Labour leader. The suspicion was that he wanted to stay in post until he was sure that neither Morrison nor Bevan would succeed him. In Attlee's eyes, only Gaitskell could replace him. Remaining at the helm did Labour no favours. The economy was booming, with full employment, higher exports and rising standards of living. The Conservatives claimed that voting Labour would mean going back to austerity, even predicting the return of the ration book. Much though the party denied these accusations, Labour's public face was Attlee's, associated with all the privations of the immediate post-war period. Wilson, back on the front bench, was used by Labour in several televised broadcasts, appearing 'forthright, unsmiling, the grim efficient executive', according to one television critic.

The Bevanites did badly, with Michael Foot losing Plymouth and Barbara Castle only scraping home in

Blackburn, but Wilson doubled his majority in Huyton. Asked to produce a post-mortem on Labour's performance, he was scathing about the inadequacy of the party's electoral machine, which he said was 'still at the penny-farthing stage in a jet-propelled era'.

The report earned him kudos, not least from the *New Statesman*, which said it had made Wilson 'a figure of political importance' and that Labour 'may have found the manager it has needed so long – young, vigorous, modern-minded and able to see that a party machine must be an inspiration to party workers and not merely a means of disciplining them'.

Wilson had managed to diminish the chances of both the men whom Attlee didn't want to succeed him: Bevan's by leaving him to stew in his own juice and Morrison's by criticising the party machine for which he'd been responsible. Attlee resigned in November. The election to replace him was held over a single week the following month. Morrison attracted the support of 40 MPs, Bevan 70, and Gaitskell won outright with 157 votes, including that of Harold Wilson. Wilson's reward was to be appointed Shadow Chancellor.

It's important to stress that there is not the slightest equivalence between a Cabinet minister and their shadow. At the Board of Trade Wilson had presided over 14,000 civil servants. For them and their colleagues the opposition didn't exist until shortly before a general election, when there was a need to ascertain what might be expected of the civil service in the event of a change of governing party. While Harold Macmillan, the Chancellor whom Wilson now shadowed, would have had all the considerable resources of Her Majesty's Treasury at his disposal, Wilson would have felt lucky to get a couple of Labour Party appointed advisors in addition to his secretary.

It was in April 1956, at a dinner in honour of Nikita Khrushchev at the House of Commons, that Harold Wilson first met that 'secretary', the woman who would become a dominant figure in his life until the day he died. To use Wilson's own autobiographical words: 'Her name was Marcia Williams. The following year she joined me as my full-time political secretary to deal with my enormous mailbag. She worked first out of my office at Montague Meyer and stayed with me through all the vicissitudes of the following twenty years.' The question that most of Wilson's biographers have grappled with is: just how many of those 'vicissitudes' were caused by the woman he was writing about?

Marcia Williams (née Field) was a country girl from Northamptonshire who'd studied history at Queen Mary College, London. There she'd met Ed Williams, who chaired the Conservative Students' Club; she was secretary of the Labour Society. By the time they married in 1955, Ed was an aerodynamics engineer whose interest in politics had faded. Marcia's hadn't. She was working as a secretary at Transport House in Smith Square, headquarters of the Labour Party, and it was her excellent shorthand that had earned an invitation to the dinner. Stalin's successor was making the first visit to London by a Russian leader since the 1917 revolution. It was an historic event, and the party wanted a record of the postprandial speeches.

What followed was a diplomatic and social disaster. Gaitskell, as Labour leader, took the opportunity to present a list of Russian social democrats being held as political prisoners. Khrushchev reacted by making a bellicose speech insisting that Russia alone had defeated Germany. George Brown, a prominent shadow cabinet member with a drink problem, interrupted with the accurate but undiplomatic observation that Britain had lost almost half a million men during the period when Stalin was still Hitler's ally. Things deteriorated from there.

Whether the Shadow Chancellor gave Marcia Williams a lift home that night is disputed, but the memorable date of the dinner (23.4.56) became significant among the people who worked closely for Wilson. Joe Haines, who later became his No. 10 press secretary, claimed that the way to induce panic in Marcia was to count loudly from two to six. He also referred to her habit of tapping her handbag meaningfully as if it contained some great secret, possibly related to that evening. If so, the secret in the handbag has never been revealed. One aspect of the speculation about the relationship between Harold and Marcia concerned the fact that Marcia's marriage didn't last. Later that same year, Ed went to work for Boeing in Seattle on a two-year contract. He never came back.

In his book about working in Downing Street, Joe Haines also says:

> [Marcia] met for a great many years a deep craving within [Wilson]: for someone else to whom politics was meat and drink and the very air that was breathed; someone who at her best had a political mind capable of testing and matching his... someone who was prepared to devote all her time to Harold Wilson's service; and someone who, at the very worst moments, was always there.

Of course, Mary was always there as well, but she had very different interests to her husband and was happy that politics rarely intruded into their domestic life. Their eldest son, Robin, can't remember a single occasion when politics was discussed around the dinner table. His mother's interests were art and literature. While she had political opinions, she found nothing compelling about the mechanics of politics or the gossip in Westminster. Perhaps that was just as well, because before too long a great deal of that gossip centred on just how close the relationship was between Harold Wilson and the woman he'd appointed as his political and personal secretary.

From the very beginning he relied on Marcia's judgement and valued her opinion. Sixteen years his junior, she gave him, he felt, a more modern perspective at a time when he was becoming increasingly focused on how to move Britain forward from its imperial past.

It was the American statesman Dean Acheson who famously said in 1962 that Great Britain had lost an empire and not yet found a role. The phrase summed up Wilson's increasing frustration with what he saw as a hopelessly out-of-date, class-bound establishment holding the country back.

He thrived as Shadow Chancellor, developing a reputation for eloquence and wit that soon had MPs flocking to the chamber whenever he spoke. And it was a good time for the party. Gaitskell's personal animosity towards Bevan softened once he became leader, and this, coupled with the shock of the 1955 defeat, spawned a truce between right and left.

Britain's humiliation in the Suez crisis fatally damaged Eden's premiership, and by January 1957 the Conservatives had a new leader. Harold Macmillan had taken over and

Labour was building a significant lead in the polls. Wilson was even more critical of Britain's incongruity as a nation after Suez, a country still in thrall to a landed gentry as the rest of the world embraced the dynamism of the scientific age. He single-handedly forced the government to instigate a tribunal of inquiry when Macmillan's successor at the Treasury, Peter Thorneycroft, was accused of leaking an increase in the bank rate to friends in the City who'd profited from the information. Despite the inquiry exonerating the minister, Wilson initiated a two-day debate in which he gave a sparkling performance, denouncing the 'casino mentality' of the City of London, espousing the causes of modernity, efficiency and science against the sclerotic influence of the old boy network. It was this speech that converted many more Labour MPs to Marcia Williams's belief that Harold Wilson was a future party leader.

13

NOBODY thought Wilson's opportunity would come for many years given Gaitskell's relative youth (he was in his early fifties) and vigour (few MPs were as energetic). Still regarded as being on the left, although no longer a Bevanite, Wilson was derided by many in Gaitskell's social set, which mainly consisted of hedonists like Roy Jenkins and Tony Crosland, who loved to gather for cocktail parties and gourmet dinners.

This wasn't something that divided Gaitskell from Bevan, a fellow bon viveur, but it separated him from Wilson, whose idea of fine dining was a cold pork pie with a glug of HP Sauce. Wilson was thought to be 'provincial' and, by the more snobbish of the Gaitskellites, 'a common little man'.

'Life's better with the Conservatives. Don't let Labour ruin it,' pronounced the Tory election slogan for the 1959 election. The economy was booming, unemployment was low and living standards were rising, allowing Macmillan to claim famously that the nation had 'never had it so good'. While 'Supermac' lacked the matinee idol looks of Sir Anthony Eden, he was a moderate one-nation Tory who'd steered his party back to popularity after the disaster of Suez. He was also one of 13 Old Etonians in a 19-man Cabinet (there were no women) that Wilson accused of having a born-to-rule mentality. Parliamentary representation would continue to exclude over 50 per cent of the population: out of 1,536 candidates at the 1959 general election, only 76 were women.

Election day on 8 October produced the most disappointing of Labour's three consecutive defeats. They were a united party under a credible leader with a consistent opinion poll lead that seemed to evaporate on contact with the electorate. The Conservative majority increased to a hundred; Labour lost 19 seats and its share of the vote fell by 2.7 per cent.

Gaitskell was quick to tell his friends that he thought Wilson's proposal to reduce purchase tax (now known as VAT) was a factor, even though he'd backed the idea and his own maladroit handling of it, giving the impression that it was an election bribe, had done more damage than the policy itself.

Party conference was held in Blackpool only a month after the election defeat. Gaitskell was convinced that his party couldn't preach modernity while being tied to a Soviet-style nationalisation model that had been incorporated into Labour's constitution in the year of the Bolshevik Revolution. It was time for the party's commitment to the mixed economy to be reflected in its rule book. Wilson, still Shadow Chancellor, felt that the offending words in Clause IV of Labour's constitution (committing the party to 'the common ownership of the means of production, distribution and exchange') was more a theoretical declaration than a policy statement. He said that asking a Labour conference to remove it would be akin to asking Christians to remove Genesis from the Bible. Privately, he told a group of journalists that 'of course' Labour didn't want to put 'every corner sweet shop and petrol station' under state control. Like many in Labour at the time, he saw Gaitskell's attempt to remove the clause as unnecessarily divisive at a time when Labour's warring factions were at peace.

Nye Bevan had been a diminished force on the left since a conference speech a few years earlier, when, as Shadow Foreign Secretary, he had argued that expecting him to support unilateral nuclear disarmament would be akin to sending him 'naked into the negotiating chamber'. Nevertheless, he was lauded at this conference for making a brilliant speech opposing his leader's proposals by equating nationalisation with socialism. It would be the charismatic Welshman's final speech to a Labour conference.

Gaitskell lost the vote. Not only did Clause IV survive, but the conference also decided to reproduce it on every membership card.

A bigger personal problem for Gaitskell was that he'd made an enemy of his Shadow Chancellor, whose unemotional, semi-detached disposition disguised a cold fury at the way his party leader was treating him. Told of Gaitskell's intention to move him from the Treasury brief, Wilson set about shoring up his position. By tradition, the powerful Public Accounts Committee of the House of Commons had always been chaired by an opposition MP, but one from the back benches, never a shadow minister, and certainly not the Shadow Chancellor. The committee had licence to ascertain if government was spending taxpayers' money appropriately.

Its chair had access to privileged and sensitive information. Taking on the role was a clever move by someone Gaitskell was forced to accept as a particularly astute politician. The *Daily Express*, still a mass-circulation newspaper, reported that 'Mr Wilson is accumulating influence and authority almost effortlessly'. The article also claimed that although Wilson was 'curiously unloved' he had become indispensable to the Labour Party.

He gave up the Montague L. Meyer job, which had been of enormous value, doing far more than maintaining the international links he'd established at the Board of Trade. With a couple of exceptions, shadow cabinet members (then as now) didn't receive a salary, and most MPs in the 1950s didn't have an office. Meyer had provided both.

The reason Wilson gave for leaving was to avoid a possible conflict of interest, but his closest allies knew it was to focus more on Westminster. Bevan's death from stomach cancer eight months after the Clause IV debate meant that the deputy leadership was now vacant. Having successfully thwarted Gaitskell's plan to downgrade him, Wilson now set his sights on becoming his deputy. He had no wish to be an heir to Bevan as some kind of spiritual leader of the left. There were no Wilsonites, but he did want to remain on good terms with Bevan's followers, to be a conciliator between the two wings of the party. There was no issue upon which conciliation was more necessary than that of Britain's nuclear deterrent.

Bevan's dramatic intervention on Gaitskell's behalf in 1958 hadn't settled the argument, and, with the Campaign for Nuclear Disarmament (CND) attracting huge support

and the unions gradually switching from supporting a negotiated disarmament among all nuclear states (multilateral
disarmament) to arguing that Britain should abandon its
nuclear deterrent as an example to others (unilateral disarmament), the 1960 conference in Scarborough looked like
being another televised display of disunity.

An attempted 'no first use' compromise wasn't good
enough for Frank Cousins, the leader of the TGWU, who'd
become the major evangelist for the unilateralists, as he had
been on retaining Clause IV. The argument became increasingly bitter as conference approached. Wilson remained
largely on its sidelines. He was a multilateralist and supporter of NATO membership, which Britain would probably
have to concede in a switch to unilateralism. But he also
felt that conference decisions should be respected, whereas
Gaitskell considered those who challenged his position to be
Communist-inspired, as indeed they may have been given that
some union delegates were CPGB members. (It wasn't until
1965 that the rules were changed to ensure that all conference
delegates had to be members of the Labour Party.)

Gaitskell lost the vote, his second defeat on a major issue
at successive conferences. The first had been on an internal
party matter; this was an important issue of government
policy. Media commentators expected it to be a resignation
issue for the leader. But Gaitskell didn't resign. Instead, he displayed a magnificent defiance, delivering his famous 'We will
fight and fight and fight again' speech and earning a standing
ovation from the conference that had only just humiliated
him – a standing ovation that Wilson conspicuously failed
to participate in. He remained seated in the fug of tobacco

smoke that in those days shrouded every conference plat-form, lighting and relighting his pipe. As the *Sunday Times* observed: 'Never have so many matches been struck in such a short time on one small pipeful of tobacco.'

The pipe smoker had been planning to be Gaitskell's deputy just as Bevan, his mentor, had been. But he knew that the leader's defiant stance was bound to attract a leadership challenge and that the press had been carefully watching his reaction precisely because they saw him as Gaitskell's successor.

He could have allowed the furore to die down, but his hand was forced when Anthony Greenwood, the Labour MP for Rossendale (and son of the wartime minister who'd commissioned the Beveridge Report), put his own name forward for leader. Gaitskell was going to be challenged, and if Wilson wasn't careful he'd lose his influence on the left while allowing the right to portray him as weak and indecisive. He put his name forward aware that he'd lose badly, and he did – by a little over two to one (161 to 81).

Wilson's status and seniority, as well as his effectiveness as a parliamentary performer, made him unsackable, but after six years on the Treasury brief, he accepted a move sideways, to be Shadow Foreign Secretary. In the 15 months that Wilson served in that position, one issue is of particular significance to his story: Britain's relationship with Europe.

In July 1961, Macmillan confirmed that Britain would apply to join the six countries who were members of what was then known officially as the European Economic Community (EEC) and, more informally, as the Common Market. This was an issue that divided Labour to a much greater extent than it did the Conservatives. Here, Gaitskell was largely in tune with the mood of his party when he declared at the 1962 conference that joining the EEC would mean Britain being absorbed into a European state and would mark 'the end of a thousand years of history'.

It was as he basked in the subsequent warm ovation that his wife, Dora, made her famous observation that all the wrong people were cheering. Having offended the left on nuclear disarmament, he now offended the right (and some of his most fervent followers) over Europe. His Shadow Foreign Secretary was more equivocal. The man who'd worked for Jean Monnet at the start of the war understood the motivation behind Monnet and Schuman's great vision of a Europe at peace but emphasised the need to wait and see what terms were being offered for Britain's membership before deciding Labour's attitude. He shared the concerns of colleagues on the left that membership would inhibit Britain's ability to plan its future but, most of all, he worried about the impact on the Commonwealth.

The Huddersfield Boy Scout who'd travelled to Australia with his mother had always had the idea of Britain's family of nations close to his heart. He wasn't a supporter of colonialism, but of the strand of the Labour left that, in his formative years, had advocated the Commonwealth as a great driver of human emancipation. The Commonwealth Labour Group could boast members like Clydeside MP Tom Johnston and former party leader George Lansbury.

Wilson's pragmatic 'wait and see' response in the parliamentary debate on Macmillan's proposal avoided an ideological split, as it would again a decade later. For now, the crocodile came nowhere near the canoe: talks on Britain's membership broke down.

The more popular Wilson became with Labour activists, the more distrusted he was by Gaitskellites and the party establishment. In October 1962 he decided to run for deputy leader against the incumbent, George Brown. While Wilson had excelled in criticising US brinkmanship in the Cuban Missile Crisis that month, Brown was losing his appeal even among his strongest supporters due to his continued heavy drinking. A revelation that he'd been secretly on the payroll of the *Daily Mirror* had also been damaging. But despite this, and Brown's enthusiastic Europhile stance in a party that was in the main Eurosceptic, he beat Wilson by 133 votes to 103. Wilson had failed to win over his parliamentary colleagues twice in two years. The received opinion was that he was an overambitious man who couldn't be trusted. 'Too clever by half' was the peculiarly British phrase used about a man who'd dared to demonstrate wit and flair in debate. Roy Hattersley, who was very much a Gaitskellite, albeit of a younger generation, thinks the clique around the leader couldn't believe that a man who'd dined at the high tables of Oxford could prefer tinned to smoked salmon. He saw Wilson as a good Labour man who despised privilege and was driven by a desire to help the disadvantaged and dispossessed.

Late in 1962, as Britain froze in the coldest winter for 200 years, Hugh Gaitskell was hospitalised by what was eventually diagnosed as lupus, a rare autoimmune disease that attacks the vital organs. He died on 18 January 1963. The two men who'd defined the opposite wings of the Labour

Party, Bevan and Gaitskell, were dead and buried within three years of each other. Given his recent victory as deputy leader, George Brown was the initial favourite to take the crown. Only two years older than Wilson, he had the Labour advantage of a more working-class background. But this was a ballot of MPs, not members, and Brown made the mistake of trying to strong-arm colleagues into supporting him. But what really ruined his chances was the intervention of a third candidate, James Callaghan. He'd succeeded Wilson as Shadow Chancellor and had all of Brown's proletarian credentials with none of the baggage. The first ballot result was Wilson 115, Brown 88, Callaghan 41. As no candidate had received the required 50 per cent of the vote, there was a second ballot in which Wilson beat Brown by 144 to 103. On Valentine's Day 1963, Harold Wilson became leader of the Labour Party and of Her Majesty's Most Loyal Opposition.

14

I T was a month later when the man who'd headed up Wilson's leadership campaign, George Wigg, Labour MP for Dudley, used parliamentary privilege to ask the Home Secretary about rumours connecting a government minister with a call girl (to use the favoured euphemism of the time), Christine Keeler. The Home Secretary refused to comment, but what had previously been gossip and press speculation (particularly in a new satirical magazine called *Private Eye*) had been transcribed into the pages of Hansard, forcing the minister concerned, John Profumo, Secretary of State for War, to respond. He issued a statement the following day, claiming that there'd been 'no impropriety whatsoever' in his relationship with Keeler, who was said by the press also to be sleeping with a Soviet naval attaché, Captain Yevgeny Ivanov. Having delivered this firm denial, Profumo took his glamorous film-star wife, Valerie Hobson, to Sandown races, where they were guests of the Queen Mother. A few months later, on 4 June, Profumo, forced to admit that he'd lied to Parliament, resigned as a minister and MP.

The priapic activities of a government minister wouldn't normally have threatened to bring down a Prime Minister. Macmillan's misfortune was that it happened when there was a yearning for change and a palpable sense that a new age was dawning. *That Was the Week That Was* was bringing *Private Eye*'s satire and irreverence to the TV screen; 'kitchen sink' films like *Room at the Top* and *This Sporting Life* were portraying working-class life as a constant battle against inherited privilege; and the defection of the spy Kim Philby had uncovered deceit and betrayal among the upper classes. The baby boom after the war had become the teenage revolution of the 1960s. Beatlemania was omnipresent in Britain as a prelude to world domination. Macmillan suddenly looked like a man out of time, the embodiment of national decay.

Wilson surfed the incoming tide. He was adroit in his handling of the Profumo scandal, which Wigg had alerted him to long before the parliamentary question had been asked, dealing with its personal aspects sensitively. 'We are not here as a court of morals,' he told Parliament in the debate that followed Profumo's departure. Seeking an independent judicial inquiry, his case against the former Secretary of State wasn't that he'd had sex with a prostitute but that 'a man in a position of high trust, privy to the most secret information available to a government, through a continuing association with this squalid network, imperilled our national security.'

Wilson got his inquiry, and when Lord Denning published his report in October 1963 the queues to buy it at HMSO were as long as they had been for Beveridge's report 20 years before.

Another important government document was published that month. Lord (Lionel) Robbins, an economist who'd advised Churchill during the war, produced his *Higher Education: Report of the Committee Appointed by the Prime Minister*, which became known as the 'Robbins Report'. In the early 1960s, a university education was the preserve of a privileged few: only around 4 per cent of youngsters entered higher education, and working-class participation was minuscule. Many in post-war Britain felt this situation to be desirable. To be clear, 96 per cent of young people weren't being excluded because they couldn't obtain the necessary qualifications: in the year preceding the report's publication, a quarter of those with the required A levels were prevented from going to university because there weren't enough places. Robbins recommended a huge expansion, establishing a principle that seems unremarkable now but was revolutionary at the time. In 26 words he sought to sweep away the elitism of the past. 'Courses of higher education,' Robbins pronounced, 'should be available for all those who are qualified by ability and attainment to pursue them and who wish to do so.' Within 24 hours the government had accepted all 178 of the report's recommendations. While it was the government who'd commissioned the report and reacted to it, Wilson had made rejection politically unthinkable. On 1 October 1963, three weeks before the Robbins Report was published, Harold Wilson had given his first speech as leader to Labour's conference in Scarborough. It is possibly the most famous and influential conference speech by any British politician and, unusually for a leader's speech, it was written entirely by the man who delivered it.

The principal message was the need to harness socialism to science and science to socialism (this was, after all, a party conference speech), but its subtext was to be the consistent theme of his leadership: that the Conservatives were incapable of facing up to the challenges of the modern age. Wilson used a cricketing analogy. 'At the very time that even the MCC has abolished the distinction between amateurs and professionals, in science and industry we are content to remain a nation of gentlemen in a world of players.'

Building upon the government's careless approach to national security exposed by the Profumo scandal, this tapped into a powerful current of public concern. Although knowing nothing of what would be in the Robbins Report, he stressed the need to create 200,000 extra university places, and was coruscating about what he termed the 'apartheid' of selective education. 'To train the scientists we are going to need will mean a revolution in our attitude to education, not only higher education but at every level... It means that, as a nation, we cannot afford to force segregation on our children at the 11+ stage.'

He attacked the snobbery of not allowing technology colleges to award degrees, called for higher education to have its own minister and, placing all this in an international context, pledged to introduce a Ministry of Overseas Development.

Another commitment was made: to introduce a 'university of the air', an open university requiring no prior attainment, specifically aimed at the millions of adults who'd been denied the opportunity to study for a degree.

To make a decent speech great requires a phrase that resonates, that captures its essence in a few words. Wilson's came near the end: 'The Britain that is going to be forged in the white heat of this revolution will be no place for restrictive practices or for outdated methods on either side of industry.'

Robert McKenzie, speaking on the BBC lunchtime news, said that Wilson had moved the Labour Party forward 50 years in 50 minutes. The 'white heat' speech cemented Wilson's popularity in the Labour Party, but more importantly it established his Prime Ministerial credentials among the public.

It was a beleaguered Conservative Party that drifted into its own conference at Blackpool the following week to hear the news that Macmillan was departing the crease. To have sent a 'gentleman' like the Fourteenth Earl of Home (who, incidentally, had been a first-class cricketer) out to replace him seems positively masochistic when there were 'players' like Rab Butler, Iain Macleod and Reginald Maudling available. But after renouncing his hereditary peerages (there were several), Sir Alec Douglas-Home hit the campaign trail in the Kinross and Western Perthshire by-election that would transfer him from the Lords to the Commons.

Wilson's first trip to America as Labour leader had been in April 1963 to meet President Kennedy; his second was to accompany Douglas-Home to the President's funeral six months later. Kennedy had been assassinated in Dallas on 22 November. At the funeral Wilson met Kennedy's successor, Lyndon Johnson, for the first time. Kennedy had been careful in his support for South Vietnam's war with the Communist North, avoiding direct military involvement. Johnson was to abandon that caution. This was the first of many occasions on which the two men would talk about Vietnam.

It was the end of 1963. An election year loomed. If he won, Wilson now knew he couldn't place his 'white heat' vision for the country in the hands of his deputy, George Brown. When they had stood for the position of party leader, Tony Crosland, a fervent Gaitskellite, described it as a choice between a crook and a drunk. While Wilson certainly wasn't a crook, the description of Brown was accurate. Never was this more apparent than on the night of Kennedy's death. Brown had been detailed to speak for the Labour Party on live TV. Clearly half-cut and slurring his words, he claimed a friendship with JFK which was toe-curlingly exaggerated. The interview inspired *Private Eye* to invent the phrase 'tired and emotional' as a euphemism for the state the deputy leader of the Labour Party was in.

Brown apologised, but with more belligerence than sincerity. Wilson decided to offer the technology role to Frank Cousins, bringing him into the Cabinet from the TGWU in the same way that Ernest Bevin had been recruited for a specific government role in the wartime coalition. The offer was made surreptitiously; Cousins accepted. It was a shrewd move, binding Labour's most important affiliate to Wilson's cause. Rather than have Brown at the proposed Ministry of Technology, Wilson planned to put him in charge of another of his innovations, the Department of Economic Affairs (DEA). One of his proud boasts when reflecting on his career was that he'd never submitted to the control of the Treasury, having 'fought them to a standstill all my political life'. Recreating the DEA that Attlee had invented for Cripps, and putting his deputy at its helm, was part of that battle. He believed that planning for an effective, growth-oriented economy would be impossible if the Treasury continued its practice of slamming on the economic brakes at the first sign of inflation. Brown's new department was to evolve a 'National Plan' for annual growth of 4 per cent and negotiate a voluntary prices and incomes policy to counter any inflationary effect. If this led to a clash with HMT, Brown's aggressive personality could be put to good use against the Chancellor rather than the Prime Minister.

But the most serious economic policy issue facing the country was Britain's exchange rate with the dollar. As Shadow Chancellor in 1961, Wilson had warned Parliament that 'a further devaluation would not be like the last one – a readjustment forced on us four years after the war... A second devaluation would be regarded all over the world as an acknowledgement of defeat, a recognition that we were not on a springboard but on a slide.' Wilson had of course been in Attlee's Cabinet during the devaluation of 1949. He remembered the assurance Sir Stafford Cripps had given the nation that it wouldn't happen again. In government he'd have to do more than warn: he'd have to decide. Many economists thought it inevitable, but Wilson, Brown and Shadow Chancellor Jim Callaghan remained unconvinced.

15

THE election was called for 15 October 1964 – the latest date allowed constitutionally. The Tories had been in power for 13 years. They'd recently been mired in scandal. Two Prime Ministers had resigned. Labour had a significant and consistent poll lead and was led by the most popular politician in the country. If Douglas-Home had been hoping the political wind would change direction, there was no sign of that happening – until the campaign began. On 30 September, National Opinion Polls (NOP) put the Conservatives three percentage points ahead. The main factor seemed to be a series of unofficial strikes, particularly in the car industry, which reminded the country of the government's warnings about Labour being subjugates of the unions. Once the strikes were settled, Labour's poll lead returned.

It had been a clean fight with no personal attacks until, on 4 October, the Tory Cabinet minister Quintin Hogg, responding to a heckle about Profumo, made a veiled reference to adulterers on Labour's front bench. He was obviously referring to Wilson. The rumour that he and Marcia Williams were having an affair had been doing the rounds in the Members' Tea Room for years. Gaitskell had remarked: 'If only it were true. It would be the one human attribute in the man.'

Hogg's comment granted the press permission to make equally implicit reference to this gossip, with *Private Eye* in the vanguard. The ambiguity of the minister's remarks ensured there was no legal redress, and an intervention by Clem (by this time Lord) Attlee attacking Hogg helped make the Harold and Marcia issue go away – for the time being.

Of more serious consequence was the race card being played by some Conservative candidates, particularly at Smethwick, where an openly racist campaign was being fought. Wilson reacted by declaring that Labour would introduce legislation to outlaw racial incitement and discrimination. Then, in election week itself, an unofficial strike on the London Underground paralysed the network for the first three days. The Labour leader described the strike as intolerable and said firmer measures were necessary to protect the public against such disputes. Racism in Smethwick and 'wildcat' industrial action in London were pointers to the major domestic issues that Wilson would try to address, with some success on race relations but disastrously in respect of unofficial strikes.

Labour secured the narrowest of victories – by just four seats (Labour 317, Conservative 304, Liberal 9). Harold Wilson went to Buckingham Palace to be appointed Prime Minister, the fifth of Elizabeth II's reign but the first not to have been privately educated. Wilson felt a genuine warmth towards the Queen, and by all accounts it was reciprocated.

According to Wilson's memoirs, Prime Minister and monarch 'just used to sit and chat'.

No doubt they would have talked about the most pressing problem the government faced, which was the economy. Wilson had been convinced that neither the government nor the Bank of England had been open about the true extent of Britain's economic woes. During the election campaign he'd made the extraordinary allegation that the Tory government was running a trade deficit of a million pounds a day. When the books were opened it turned out to be more than double that – a deficit on overseas payments of £800 million.

The pound had been pegged to the dollar at $2.80 ever since the 1949 devaluation, and there was a strong argument for an immediate devaluation. Many economists of left, right and centre made that argument, but the three men who mattered – Wilson, Callaghan and Brown – remained implacable. Wilson was worried that an immediate devaluation would define him as impulsive and unwilling to work at more complex solutions. In the event, thanks to a 15 per cent tariff on imports and the Bank of England securing $3 billion of credit from foreign central banks, the crisis passed. By 1965 the balance-of-payments deficit had halved.

When Wilson paid his first Prime Ministerial visit to America, one of his objectives was to secure continued US backing for sterling and the support of President Johnson for Britain's policy towards Rhodesia (now Zimbabwe), a self-governing British colony where a white supremacist, Ian Smith, had been elected to lead the country on a platform of complete independence. (The electorate was restricted to the 230,000 white settlers among an African population of

4 million.) What the President wanted in return for American support on Rhodesia was British 'boots on the ground' in Vietnam. As the US Secretary of State, Dean Rusk, complained to the American editor of *The Times*, in a comment that, were it made today, would be described as 'Trumpian': 'All we needed was one regiment. The Black Watch would have done. Just one regiment, but you wouldn't. Well don't expect us to save you again. They can invade Sussex and we wouldn't do a damn thing about it.'

As this diatribe makes clear, Wilson stood his ground. There has been much retrospective appreciation of the British lives Harold Wilson saved by keeping this country out of the Vietnam debacle (although this didn't spare him the wrath of our anti-war protesters at the time), but Wilson also saved lives in Rhodesia. From the very beginning of the crisis, he came under pressure at least to use the threat of military action to dissuade Smith from committing a treasonable act. Wilson refused, stating: 'Britain does not believe in the use of military force to settle constitutional disputes.' He was concerned that the result in landlocked Rhodesia 'would be incalculable death and destruction'.

He nevertheless convinced the President to support Britain on Rhodesia, with Johnson no doubt hoping that military assistance in Vietnam was pending.

Marcia Williams was now the Prime Minister's personal and political secretary, yet the civil service refused to allow her to accompany Wilson on the trip to America, since she was classified as a political appointee rather than a civil servant. If in the future the Prime Minster should be accompanied by his wife, they advised, Marcia could go as Mary's maid.

She may have lost that skirmish, but Marcia won a more important battle. She succeeded in establishing her office in what had previously been a waiting area next to the Cabinet Room in 10 Downing Street. Wilson, like virtually all Prime Ministers, used the Cabinet Room as his office, and Marcia managed to position herself as his praetorian guard. And she won another battle: to see all the Prime Minister's correspondence rather than just that relating to Huyton and his position as leader of the Labour Party. The Cabinet Secretary (Sir Burke Trend), having made the original decree, was forced to back down.

Political commentators place a curious emphasis on the first hundred days of a new administration, as if they had greater significance than, say, the first 86 or 250. Within the hallowed hundred-day time span, Barbara Castle had taken charge at the new Ministry of Overseas Development, as had George Brown at Economic Affairs. Brown had already unveiled a statement on productivity, prices and incomes signed by the TUC and the main employers' organisations. The National Plan for a growth rate of 4 per cent a year was emerging. In the New Year Honours there was a knighthood for Stanley Matthews, the first honour explicitly awarded for 'services to football'.

The hundredth day itself, 24 January 1965, acquired a separate and more profound significance. It was the day Winston Churchill died. The great war leader who'd dominated twentieth-century politics was 91, but that didn't lessen the nation's grief or sense of loss at his passing. There was a state funeral, which provided an opportunity for the Prime Minister to meet Ian Smith in person. Several proposed solutions were offered, including a referendum of all Rhodesians and a Royal Commission led by Smith's own chief justice. Smith refused to compromise, and, on 11 November 1965, made his 'Unilateral Declaration of Independence' (UDI). The UN Security Council declared it illegal and called upon Britain to end the rebellion. Again, Wilson rejected military intervention, relying instead on stringent economic sanctions, the withdrawal of aid and an oil embargo. He applied all his considerable problem-solving skills to the quest for majority rule in Rhodesia. Two meetings with Smith would take place at sea, on HMS *Tiger* in December 1966 and HMS *Fearless* in October 1968, all to no avail. Smith's treacherous regime would remain in place for another 14 years. While the long struggle with Smith enhanced Wilson's already wide experience of the geopolitical, it destroyed his vision of a widening and deepening relationship between Britain and the Commonwealth.

Labour's tiny majority meant that this first Wilson government was always insecure. A couple of Labour rebels could lose them a vote or force a change of policy, as happened when Wilson had to drop steel nationalisation from his first Queen's Speech. Even with these restrictions, by the end of 1965 the death penalty had been effectively abolished and a new criminal offence of incitement to racial hatred created, and measures such as the breathalyser and compulsory seat belts were being introduced (by Barbara Castle, who'd been moved to Transport) to tackle the carnage on Britain's roads.

The Conservatives, meanwhile, had a new leader. It's fair to say that it was Wilson's trenchant criticism, as well as his popularity, that forced the Tories to change the way they elected their leader and influenced who they chose. Tory MPs elected the 49-year-old, state-educated Ted Heath. The party wouldn't be led by another Old Etonian for 40 years.

Heath and Wilson were to spend a decade and four general elections opposing one another. The Beatles immortalised them on 'Taxman', the opening track of *Revolver*, and in the year preceding the album's release it was announced that the band would be awarded MBEs for services to British exports. While ostensibly Her Majesty's Birthday Honours, they were made at the behest of the Prime Minister. Harold Wilson had already managed to associate himself with the 'Fab Four' as Leader of the Opposition, when he'd convinced the chairman of EMI to let him present them with their Variety Club Show Business Personalities of 1963 award on the flimsy qualification that Ringo was a constituent. The Beatles may have been admirers of Mr Wilson, as they'd professed to be that night, but it's doubtful that this was reciprocated. Harold remained more Gilbert and Sullivan than Lennon and McCartney, but he grasped the opportunity to embellish his 'man of the people' credentials – and he was, of course, a Merseyside MP.

By December 1965 Labour had a six-point poll lead, and Wilson was more popular than his party with a 60 per cent approval rating. At conference that year, Harold's father, Herbert, made an appearance to mark his eighty-second birthday. Ethel had died of cancer in 1957. She never lived to see the son she'd taken on the long journey to Australia become Prime Minister.

When Harold Wilson told the press lobby that 'a week is a long time in politics' it was to stress how quickly political fortunes could change rather than express a preference for short-termism. He knew the poll lead could evaporate in an instant, and he now had the power to choose the date of the next election. Heath's short honeymoon period with the voters seemed to be over. While the Conservative leader came from a similar lower-middle-class background, he lacked Wilson's relaxed charm. Having publicly ruled out an election in 1965, Wilson was keeping a careful eye on a by-election in Hull North due on 27 January 1966. Henry Solomons, who'd narrowly won the seat for Labour in 1964, died *in situ*. The government's majority in the House was down to one. Labour threw everything at the campaign, even bringing Barbara Castle to Hull to promise a bridge across the Humber. Kevin McNamara duly won with a swing big enough to convince Wilson to call a general election for 31 March.

The Hull North result had accurately reflected the mood of the nation. In the election campaign a united Labour Party emphasised its greatest asset: the Prime Minister. One poster consisted simply of a pipe in an ashtray and a phrase lifted from a popular beer advertisement: 'By golly he does you good.' Labour won 363 seats and an overall majority of 97. After an 18-month apprenticeship, Harold Wilson had an unquestionable mandate to govern for the remainder of the decade.

16

THE problem of an overvalued currency had been ameliorated rather than resolved. A strike by the National Union of Seamen (NUS) in support of a pay claim that would have breached the voluntary agreement on wages and prices gave the government an opportunity to prove their commitment to the policy while also demonstrating that they could stand up to the unions. The strike began in May and didn't end until July. In between there'd been a state of emergency, a court of inquiry and a claim by Wilson that the strike was being prosecuted by 'a tightly knit group of politically motivated men'. His allegation was that the NUS was being run by Communists, which was not only unwise but inaccurate. There were undoubtedly Communists seeking influence among the seafarers, as there were in most trade unions, but Wilson had become over-influenced by the security service's myopic view. Or, to put it another way, there was a 'danger that the government would look at these problems through Communist eyes as we were forced to do', and therefore pay insufficient attention to factors beyond MI5's remit, as an agent remarked in Christopher Andrew's authorised history of the service. There had always been tension on the left between the democratic socialists of the Labour Party and the various revolutionary cliques who despised Labour but envied its influence in working-class communities. Labour had to be constantly on guard against 'entryism' by such groups. Wilson had never been a Communist or even a fellow traveller. He believed that state planning could be combined with free choice, social discipline with civil liberty, a strong executive with independent justice. While he recognised Labour's enduring dilemma of how to speak persuasively for the poor, as well as for the more prosperous and the socially mobile, he was convinced that if the party could align itself with the public's thirst for change and modernity it had a unique opportunity to become the natural party of government as the Conservatives had been throughout most of the post-war period.

Wilson didn't give in to the NUS, but his prices and incomes policy had only been protected at the cost of another sterling crisis. Frank Cousins ended his unhappy second-ment from the TGWU, in part because of what he saw as the government's intransigence over the strike, but mainly because of his attachment to the principle of 'free collective bargaining'. Those three words had a strange, almost mystic, hold on the British trade union movement. They were isolated among trade unionists in Europe by opposing a national minimum wage, a minimum holiday entitlement or any legal restriction on the number of hours an employee could be made to work. These issues were to be determined between unions and employers through negotiation (aka free collective bargaining). The departure of Cousins, coming after the destructive seamen's strike, focused attention back on the issue upon which Labour was most vulnerable: increasing union militancy. There were too many unions competing for membership, with internal union squabbles causing some of the disputes. Wilson, a supporter of free trade unionism, wanted to extend its influence through industrial democracy, introducing a right for workers to have a meaningful say in how their industries were run. This was something else that was popular on the Continent but anathema to most British trade unions at the time. The TUC, more sympathetic to such ideas, had called for a Royal Commission on the relationship between employers and unions, which Wilson originally rejected, telling the first congress he'd attended as Prime Minister that such commissions worked at a snail's pace, 'taking minutes and wasting years'. But he changed his mind, appointing a High Court judge, Lord Donovan, to chair a commission which did indeed take years, reporting eventually in 1968. But in the wake of the seamen's strike its establishment helped stabilise the government's relationship with the unions, allowing Wilson to concentrate on the continuing problem of an overvalued currency.

By early July, the Bank of England was burning through its reserves to try to stabilise the pound against an intensification of short selling. George Brown, still a volatile presence at Economic Affairs, now argued that without devaluation the National Plan was doomed. Callaghan, as Chancellor of the Exchequer, was wavering. Of the three main players, only Wilson remained firmly against devaluing the pound. He made clear to Cabinet, the Bank of England and the Treasury that the government must pursue every alternative so that, if devaluation became necessary, the world would appreciate that it hadn't been adopted as an easy way out. At a crunch meeting of the Cabinet, Brown threatened to resign if Wilson adopted deflationary policies such as a wage freeze. Richard Crossman and Roy Jenkins (now Home Secretary) argued for devaluation, as did Barbara Castle, but Wilson won the vote, 17–6. Moves to dampen demand were implemented, including a six-month pay and prices freeze, which provoked yet another resignation threat by Brown.

England's victory in the World Cup final on 30 July provided some cheerful relief. Wilson attended the celebration dinner at the Royal Garden Hotel that evening, no doubt delighted that at left back in the winning team was a Wilson who played for Huddersfield Town. George Brown was with him at the celebration, leading a table of West Ham supporters in a rendition of 'I'm Forever Blowing Bubbles'.

Brown's attempt to burst Wilson's bubble got him promoted. Knowing his deputy had always coveted the position of Foreign Secretary (and possibly remembering how Attlee had dealt with a mutinous Cripps), Wilson offered him the job, thus reducing Brown's ability to cause trouble domestically by transferring him to an international brief. An important part of this role would be to oversee a bid to join the Common Market which Wilson now planned to submit. However, the French Prime Minister, Georges Pompidou, had already stated his view that for any British application to stand a chance of succeeding, the pound would need to be devalued. The application was eventually submitted on 10 May 1967, a few days after 74 Labour MPs signed a statement declaring that the Treaty of Rome was about free markets and would destroy any likelihood of a planned economy. That had always been Wilson's view, but although he was yet to become as committed a European as Ted Heath, he recognised the significant economic advantages of joining the customs union. He couldn't help but be aware of the fervent support for Britain's entry among Cabinet colleagues such as Jenkins, Crosland and Brown. He'd pleased them by submitting the application but kept Eurosceptics on side by stressing that the final decision would depend on the terms negotiated. In the event it took the French President, Charles de Gaulle, just six days to give a firm *non* to Britain's application.

By the end of 1967, after an unofficial docks strike, and with a rising trade deficit and falling exports, sterling was once again under severe pressure. According to Richard Crossman, Wilson was under so much strain that he was drinking whisky at Cabinet meetings. On 11 November he met with Callaghan and Brown. Now all three men saw devaluation as the only feasible option. At Cabinet five days later, Callaghan warned that any attempt to maintain parity would exhaust the already depleted reserves, and it was agreed that, in two days' time, on Saturday, 18 November, our currency would move to a new fixed parity of $2.40 to the pound, down from the $2.80 applied in 1949. A Prime Ministerial TV broadcast on Friday evening would convey this to the public. It was the broadcast that arguably inflicted more damage on the government than the policy itself. Its purpose was to try to avoid the panic of 18 years previously, when worried citizens had tried to withdraw their money from banks, convinced that each pound was about to be reduced to 17 shillings. Back then, few people had television;

now it was ubiquitous, and the devaluation was 14 rather than 30 per cent. What could possibly go wrong?

Wilson's Treasury draft had him saying: 'This does not mean that the money in our pockets is worth 14 per cent less to us now,' but he changed it to: 'This doesn't mean, of course, that the pound here in Britain, in your pocket or purse or in your bank, has been devalued.' Although this was technically correct – £100 savings pre-devaluation would remain £100 – what that money could purchase in goods and currency from abroad had been diminished. Ted Heath latched on to this, telling the Commons that Wilson's broadcast 'will be remembered as the most dishonest statement ever made... even by the Prime Minister'. In fact, Wilson had made clear elsewhere in the broadcast that purchasing goods from abroad would be more expensive, stressing 'higher prices for imports'. But this was a case of Wilson being too clever by half. Had he left the Treasury script unchanged it may still have led to accusations of dishonesty, but undoubtedly it was the more alliterative terminology of 'the pound in your pocket' that did the damage. He was also criticised for his jaunty tone, as if talking about some great battle he'd won rather than a war of attrition that he'd lost. Devaluation marked the moment when the popular perception of the Prime Minister changed, from avuncular statesman to devious and manipulative schemer. After the 'pound in your pocket' broadcast it was never glad confident morning again for James Harold Wilson.

17

CALLAGHAN had made it clear that he couldn't continue as Chancellor if sterling was devalued. It wasn't a resignation threat: Callaghan supported the policy but felt its necessity reflected a Treasury failing for which he should take responsibility. Rather than lose him to the back benches, Wilson arranged a job swap with the Home Secretary. Roy Jenkins's two-year stint at the Home Office had allowed the son of a Welsh miner to pursue the liberalising policies he had long advocated. Capital punishment had ended, as had the birching of young offenders; homosexuality had been decriminalised, and divorce made easier. Abortion law was liberalised, and theatre censorship ended. These were radical societal changes that now define the decade. For those wedded to the status quo, however, they represented a descent into depravity, with discipline and restraint giving way to the lechery and immorality of the 'permissive society'. Wilson's biographer, Ben Pimlott, summarised Jenkins's motivation beautifully. It was 'to end a variety of judicial persecutions of private behaviour; quietly to consolidate a mood change in British society;

and to provide a legal framework for more civilised social values'.

These liberal reforms are sometimes attributed to the MPs who championed their cause in Private Members' Bills (such as David Steel on abortion). But if Roy Jenkins hadn't thrown the government's support behind them they would have had no chance of making it onto the statute books. Jenkins was undoubtedly a great Home Secretary. But he could not have succeeded without Prime Ministerial support. Wilson was an implacable opponent of racial prejudice (on which Jenkins began the process of enhancing the 1965 legislation) but more circumspect on abortion rights and the legalisation of homosexuality. This is understandable in the context of the profound influence the Catholic Church wielded, particularly in the north-west, where Wilson was an MP. There was good reason to proceed with caution, but proceed Wilson did.

Roy Jenkins had been one of Gaitskell's most devoted disciples, but he had much more in common with Bevanite Wilson. Both were grammar-school boys who went to Oxford, although Jenkins was undoubtedly an apple that fell much further from the tree: in his speech, his mannerisms and his epicurean devotion to food and wine, he seemed almost from a different species. Balliol and the friendships he cultivated had provided a passport to an inner circle that Wilson never acquired (nor desired). But despite their differences, Wilson liked Jenkins, recognised his capabilities, and admired the skill and confidence with which he performed his ministerial duties. As Chancellor in the wake of devaluation he would need all those abilities to steady the ship in the most hostile conditions the Wilson government had faced.

By February 1968, the Tories were 22 points ahead in the polls; three months later the gap had increased to 28. In the meantime, George Brown, like Bevan before him, submitted one resignation threat too many. Although out of government, he would remain deputy leader until the 1970 general election, in which he lost his seat. Wilson's personal rating fell by 30 points (although at +27 it remained high compared with the ratings of more recent Prime Ministers). With his 1966 mandate intact for three more years, he focused attention on his most difficult challenge: trade union reform.

Fewer than half of trade unions were affiliated to the Labour Party, but those unions would make this an issue capable of dividing Labour to an even greater degree than it divided the country. Wilson recognised that for unions to be able to stop spontaneous, 'unofficial' walkouts engineered by local shop stewards, regulation would be necessary to delay and defuse such disputes. He promoted Barbara Castle to introduce these reforms as Employment Secretary. She published a white paper in January 1969 entitled *In Place of Strife*, in a nod towards Nye Bevan's influential book *In Place of Fear*.

The proposals seem mild today, set against the measures that were eventually introduced by the Thatcher government of the 1980s. There were powers to require pre-strike ballots, to order a 28-day cooling-off period and to impose a settlement if the industrial action stemmed from an inter-union dispute. Separately, via the recommendations of the Donovan Commission, workers would be given a more meaningful say in how their industries were run. Wilson felt he had public support for government intervention into what was becoming a chaotic and almost anarchic national embarrassment. This public support included most trade unionists. Unfortunately, it didn't include Wilson's Home Secretary, James Callaghan, a former trade union official. Bitterly opposed to any government intervention, when a colleague suggested to him that reform was not only necessary but inevitable, Callaghan replied, 'Okay, if it's inevitable, let the Tories pass it. All I'm saying is it's not our issue.' In the titanic clash that followed, the unions won. The Industrial Relations Bill was humiliatingly withdrawn in favour of a 'solemn and binding' undertaking by the TUC to put their house in order. No effective change was made, and ten years later Callaghan's period as Wilson's successor in Downing Street was to end in the wake of the so-called 'Winter of Discontent'. In 1969 the number of working days lost through industrial action was 6,846,000. Ten years later it was 29,474,000. Contrary to Callaghan's assertion, it had been Labour's issue, and failure to resolve it damaged the party and the unions, whose membership halved within two decades.

There was nothing underhand or devious in the way Harold Wilson dealt with the issue of trade union reform. He was bold in his argument and unstinting in his support for Barbara Castle. With the whips identifying 150 potential rebels on Labour's benches, the TUC commitment (mercilessly pilloried by the press as the intervention of 'Mr Solomon Binding') was seen as a reasonable compromise. Given Labour's travails and Callaghan's open rebellion over *In Place of Strife*, it was hardly surprising that rumours spread about a possible coup against the party leader. At a 1969 May Day rally in the Royal Festival Hall, Wilson dealt brilliantly with this speculation by turning it into a joke.

'I know what's going on,' he told his audience, pausing for effect. 'I'm going on.' The mood lightened in the hall, as it did in the country over the following year. As Chancellor, Jenkins dealt adroitly with the fallout from devaluation, introducing a series of tough measures in what he termed 'two years of hard slog'. By August, there was a £40 million surplus in the balance of payments, and this reached £387 million by the end of the year. The electorate approved of the way the government had restored financial stability as well as its reaction to events in Northern Ireland. That summer 300 troops had been sent to protect the Catholic community in Londonderry/Derry against Unionist violence. Downing Street issued an assurance that the troops would be withdrawn as soon as law and order had been restored.

But it was an issue about which the electorate knew nothing that was causing palpitations in No. 10. Marcia Williams, having given birth secretly to one child in 1968, was pregnant again. If the public did know, they would probably have a stab at guessing who the father was – and they would have been wrong. Speculation about Harold and Marcia was rife, seeping into popular culture every now and then. In an episode of *Steptoe and Son* the son, Harold Steptoe, is taken to bed by a woman whose husband is in prison. It was no coincidence that the name of Harold's fictional seductress was Marcia. In 1967 a Birmingham band called the Move hired a Soho publicist to promote their new single 'Flowers in the Rain'. The publicist commissioned a cartoon depicting a naked Harold Wilson in bed with his secretary. Five hundred postcards with this image were distributed to disc jockeys, journalists and other influential people. The postcard had nothing to do with the lyrics of the song, and the Move, away touring at the time, apparently knew nothing about the publicity stunt. Wilson sued and won. All costs had to be paid by the defendants, and the royalties from 'Flowers in the Rain' and its B-side were donated to two charities chosen by Wilson and Williams. It was estimated that the National Spastics Society (now known as Scope) and the amenity fund at Stoke Mandeville Hospital would benefit by between £2,000 and £8,000. In fact, the payments, which only ceased in 2019 when Marcia died, amounted to over a quarter of a million pounds. As if this story wasn't astonishing enough already, the QC who represented the Prime Minister in court (and who warned that the character of this libel was sufficient to have warranted criminal proceedings) was the Conservative MP and moonlighting Shadow Home Secretary, Quintin Hogg – the man whose response to a heckler at the 1964 election had helped fuel the innuendo about Harold and Marcia.

A codicil to this story concerns another Wilson reform. The explosion of pop culture and the BBC's monopoly had led to the emergence of pirate radio stations such as Radio Caroline, anchored in international waters and serving an estimated audience of 15 million listeners. Labour's Marine and Broadcasting Offences Act put most of the pirates out of business, and the BBC was forced to restructure to satisfy public demand for non-stop pop music. At 7 a.m. on 30 September 1967, Tony Blackburn played the first record on the newly created Radio 1 – 'Flowers in the Rain' by the Move, providing another royalty to Harold and Marcia's chosen charities.

Marcia gave birth to Timothy in 1968, and, in 1969, to Daniel. A large overcoat worn in the office and long periods of working from home meant that even those who worked with her in Wilson's 'kitchen cabinet' had no idea she was pregnant. An operation worthy of MI5 maintained the secrecy after Marcia's sons were born. The security service wasn't involved but it did express concern when told that the father was Walter Terry, the political editor of the *Daily Mail*.

The security service advised the Prime Minister to sack Williams because of the obvious risk that sensitive information would leak to a national newspaper. Wilson rejected the advice, and the two boys spent their early childhood living in secret. The love affair ended in 1971, when Terry returned to his wife. Not a word about any of this appeared in print. As Andrew Roth observed sagely in his biography of Wilson, perhaps this was because, while fearless in exposing the indiscretions of politicians, Fleet Street was more passive when it involved one of their own.

Was there ever a sexual relationship between Harold and Marcia? Wilson has many biographers; Marcia has only one. In *Marcia Williams: The Life and Times of Baroness Falkender* (as she was to become), Linda McDougall reveals the crucial role that Marcia played in Wilson's success and stresses how difficult it was back then for any woman to be taken seriously in politics. She repeats the anecdote of Joe Haines, Wilson's No. 10 press secretary, about Marcia confronting poor Mary Wilson to tell her she'd had sex with her husband six times in 1956, adding that 'it wasn't satisfactory'. McDougall concludes that they did have a sexual relationship, or at least that 'it is difficult to believe it never happened', but that, by the time Wilson entered 10 Downing Street, it 'was long over'.

18

18

THE only general election that Wilson lost was the one he was most confident of winning. His Chancellor's 'two years of hard slog' meant unpopular but necessary decisions being made: the withdrawal of British troops east of Suez, a 3.5 per cent limit on pay increases, the reintroduction of prescription charges, postponing the increase in the school-leaving age to 16. Labour's fortunes were inextricably linked to the post-devaluation performance of the economy, and the summer of 1969 had brought clear signs of recovery. There was a huge rise in exports and Wilson's approval rating rose with them. His legacy was beginning to emerge. The Open University, brought to life by Bevan's widow Jennie Lee, had received its royal charter in April; the higher-education expansion prescribed by Robbins was taking place; and the names of 3 million youngsters had been added to the electoral register when Britain became the first major democratic nation to lower its voting age from 21 to 18. The number of new housing completions reached 400,000 in 1968, a figure never matched before or since, and tangible evidence of the technological revolution was emerging in the nuclear reactor at Dounreay, advanced carbon fibres and a new antibiotic.

Jenkins's 1970 Budget revealed a balance-of-payments surplus, and, a week later, Labour had its first poll lead since devaluation. When Wilson called the election for 18 June, Ladbrokes offered 20 to one against a Conservative victory. Harold campaigned with Mary at his side. She was unquestionably a major asset, but her omnipresence in this campaign was probably meant to emphasise Heath's bachelor status. Then, on the Monday of election week, a setback. The trade figures for May were published, showing a £31 million deficit. The polls narrowed, but Labour retained its lead and Wilson, usually a Jeremiah at election time, remained confident of victory. It was a confidence that was misplaced. The Conservatives won with an overall majority of 30.

At 54 years of age, Wilson's eviction from Downing Street left him virtually homeless. He and Mary had sold the house in Hampstead Garden Suburb and only owned a holiday bungalow on St Mary's in the Isles of Scilly. Heath offered Chequers to get them through their first weekend out of office, and within a fortnight they'd purchased Grange Farm (a house rather than a farm) in nearby Great Missenden. Although devastated by defeat, Wilson never contemplated resigning as Labour leader. Needing a London base, they acquired a Georgian terraced town house in Lord North Street – a ten-minute stroll from Parliament and even closer to Transport House, still the shared HQ of the Labour Party and the TGWU.

There was no challenge for the party leadership but, with George Brown gone, the position of deputy leader was vacant. When Barbara Castle announced her intention to stand, Wilson dissuaded her. He had the good sense to avoid a friend and ally being his number two: much better to have somebody who attracted a different following. His preference was for Roy Jenkins, who'd impressed him even more as Chancellor than he had as Home Secretary.

Europe had again become the predominant issue. De Gaulle, having lost a referendum on French constitutional change, had resigned the presidency in April and died in October. The major opposition to British membership died with him. Jenkins was the most fervent of Labour's Europhiles, and, although the party was in opposition, Wilson knew that their position on an issue that transcended party politics on all sides of the House would be crucial.

Having identified himself with Gaitskell's anti-European rhetoric in the early 1960s, Wilson's journey from Commonwealth to Common Market was now complete. Labour was moving in the opposite direction. With Heath preparing to apply for EEC membership, Wilson faced the task of holding his party together.

Tony Benn, still very much a Wilson protégé, floated the idea of a referendum. 'I understand you are suggesting a plebiscite on the Common Market,' Wilson told him sternly one day. 'You can't do that.' This gut reaction was similar to Attlee's when Churchill had proposed a referendum to extend the life of the wartime coalition, although the then Labour leader had put it more eloquently, refusing to 'consent to the introduction into our national life of a device so alien to all our traditions as the referendum, which has only too often been the instrument of Nazism and fascism'.

But Britain had never before considered pooling its sovereignty, which the trading arrangements of the Common Market would require. Benn may have been rebuked for his temerity, but a seed had been planted.

Convinced of the futility of even attempting to knock the shine off Heath's election victory, Wilson devoted the immediate post-election period to writing a record of his time as Prime Minister. In five months he'd written an astonishing half a million words of what was to be *The Labour Government 1964–1970*. The *Sunday Times* paid £224,000 for the serialisation, money Wilson badly needed. At the time opposition parties had no access to public funds. Aside from a puny contribution from the Labour Party, Wilson had to finance his private office – the secretaries, researchers and advisors – from his own pocket. A fortnight's speaking tour of America paid the salary of Joe Haines, who'd left the No. 10 press office to work for him.

It was Haines who convinced his boss to participate in a BBC documentary about how the Wilson Cabinet had settled into opposition. Broadcast to coincide with the publication of the book in 1971, the programme's title, *Yesterday's Men*, was provocative enough. The BBC justified it by pointing out that it was the phrase Labour had used about the Conservatives in the election. The presenter, David Dimbleby, pushed the provocation further by asking Wilson how much he'd earned from the book. Wilson, usually so serene in front of the cameras, raged at Dimbleby's impertinence and complained that the BBC should be asking how a politician could afford to buy a yacht, a reference to Heath's love of sailing.

Lord Goodman, whose litigation in defence of Wilson's reputation was usually directed at purveyors of sexual innuendo, was called into action. The BBC's director general, Charles Curran, ordered the deletion of Dimbleby's question and Wilson's fiery response before the programme could be broadcast. Wilson never allowed David Dimbleby to interview him again.

Harold's wasn't the first book written by a member of the Wilson family to go on sale in the 1970s. Mary was an accomplished poet. The condescension she endured from her detractors was outweighed by the appreciation of her work expressed by distinguished poets such as Sir John Betjeman and Hugh MacDiarmid, who befriended and defended her. A book of poetry is considered a success if it sells between 50 and 250 copies. Mary Wilson's *Selected Poems* (dedicated 'To my husband'), published in 1970, recorded sales of 75,000. The royalties paid off the mortgage on the Scillies bungalow.

Being Leader of the Opposition again after six years in power must have been thoroughly depressing for a man so used to success. After a period of purdah, Wilson began to pursue his final ambition – a triumphant return to 10 Downing Street. Realising that he needed to rebuild his relationship with the unions, he pledged to repeal Heath's Industrial Relations Act 1971, which had set up a 'National Industrial Relations Court'. He then began a series of discussions with the TUC that led to the 'Social Contract', offering food subsidies and a rent freeze in return for voluntary wage restraint. He also produced a 15-point plan on the Irish situation, in which a reunified Ireland would join the Commonwealth. It had no chance of success, but, as Tony

Benn observed, Wilson's intervention 'completely defused Ireland as far as the party was concerned'.

Europe remained his biggest headache. The 1970 Labour conference rejected British entry to the Common Market by five to one. The PLP came out against it by two to one. Wilson stuck to his 'wait and see what terms are negotiated' position, but in the autumn of 1972 those terms for Britain's membership were finalised. It was crunch time. It wasn't difficult to find points of contention, and Wilson alighted on two: sugar and butter, a sweet combination to which he added a savoury constitutional objection. The Conservative manifesto had only committed Heath to negotiations on entry to the Common Market, 'no more, no less'. Beyond that, he had no mandate. Wilson made much of this in the Commons debate in an attempt to dissuade his own side from voting with the Tories.

But 69 Labour rebels, led by Jenkins, ensured that the government won the day by 356 votes to 244. Britain would join the Common Market. The dilemma now for Wilson was how to prevent Labour making a manifesto pledge to withdraw.

Tony Benn's idea seemed increasingly attractive. James Callaghan had perceptively called Benn's referendum plan 'a rubber dinghy into which we may all one day have to climb'. The dinghy was now looking very much like a Labour lifeboat.

While Benn was part of the solution on Europe, he had, as Wilson pithily remarked, 'immatured with age'. Previously a moderate voice on the Labour benches, he'd voted for Gaitskell against Bevan in the 1950s, stating that what he found 'particularly obnoxious' was the 'complacent

assumptions by the Bevanites that the ark of the socialist cov-
enant resides with them'. Many in the Labour Party would
feel that this was equally true of the Bennites 30 years later.
But in the early 1970s Benn was just beginning his transfor-
mation from Lafayette to Robespierre, and his referendum
idea was given greater legitimacy when Pompidou announced
that the enlargement of the EEC to include Britain would be
put to a referendum in France. Given his party's clear anti-
EEC stance, Wilson knew that shifting his position towards
a referendum would lead to accusations of duplicity. He
confided to Barbara Castle: 'The press will crucify me. But
I will bring the party out of this united.'

He was right about the vilification. Even the *New
Statesman* thundered its disapproval, claiming that Wilson's
'very presence in Labour's leadership pollutes the atmosphere
of politics'. It's hard to understand such a hysterical reaction
from this distance, but for the anti-marketeers Wilson was
flouting a conference decision and for Europhiles he was
threatening Britain's place in a community that he himself
had applied to join as Prime Minister.

Jenkins stepped down as deputy leader and other shadow
ministers resigned, but the 'rubber dinghy' kept Labour afloat
and they weren't at sea for as long as expected. In 1973 Ted
Heath made his biggest mistake. In November the NUM had
begun an overtime ban in support of a pay claim. A month
earlier the Yom Kippur War in the Middle East had sparked
an international oil crisis. On 13 December Heath declared
a state of emergency which included a three-day working
week to save energy and a curfew on TV broadcasts after
10.30 p.m. The dispute with the miners escalated to an all-out

strike. While the public were generally hostile to strikers, the miners fell into a different category. Not only were they respected for the difficult and dangerous nature of their work, the NUM rule book insisted on a ballot to authorise any industrial action and even stipulated a threshold that had to be met. Their leader was Joe Gormley, a Lancastrian who exuded down-to-earth common sense.

Heath's great error wasn't the state of emergency or his reaction to the NUM pay claim. It was his decision to call, with 18 months of his mandate still to run, a snap election for 28 February 1974, with the stated objective of deciding 'who governs Britain'.

The electorate decided it wouldn't be Ted Heath, but only just. Like Labour in 1951, the Tories won the popular vote (by 11.87 million to 11.65 million), but lost the election by four seats. Heath's attempt to form a coalition with the Liberals (offering their leader Jeremy Thorpe the position of Home Secretary) over that weekend failed, and Harold Wilson was back in power.

Given the narrowness of the victory, it's easy to give credence to Enoch Powell's claim that he'd tipped the balance of power towards Labour. On the Saturday before polling day, Powell, who had been a political pariah since his racist 'rivers of blood' speech in 1968 and was in political transition from Conservative to Ulster Unionist, said he was hoping for a Labour victory because of their commitment to a referendum on Europe. Two days later he urged his supporters to act accordingly. Powell later revealed that all this had been prearranged in a series of clandestine meetings with Wilson that took place in the only location where their presence together wouldn't attract suspicion: the gents toilet of the voting lobby to the right of the Speaker's chair. There was an increase in the Labour vote in those parts of the Midlands where Powell drew significant support, but whether Powell's endorsement of Labour or a trade deficit of £383 million announced on the Monday of election week sealed Heath's fate is impossible to discern.

Victory rejuvenated Harold Wilson. The journalist Mary Kenny, who'd accompanied him on the campaign trail, remarked that 'it was like watching a flower parched of water grow suddenly with the spring rain'.

19

W ITH such a slim majority, a second election was on the cards. Most commentators expected it to coincide with the lighter summer evenings. Restored and revitalised, the Prime Minister set off at a fearsome pace, which did indeed suggest that he had June in mind: on 6 March the miners' strike was settled (with a 32 per cent pay increase); on 7 March three-day-week restrictions were allowed to lapse; and on 11 March the state of emergency was lifted. But the prospect of a rapid re-engagement with the electorate was scuppered by one of Harold Macmillan's famous 'events'.

Sometimes in politics a full-blown scandal erupts from nowhere only to disappear as quickly as it emerged, leaving the public wondering what the hell it was all about. So it was with the so-called 'land deal affair'. A Wolverhampton insurance broker, Ronald Milhench, bought some contaminated land in Lancashire, producing a letter to assure potential investors of his ability to raise the necessary finance to clear the slag and stone. The land was sold by Tony Field, Marcia Williams's brother (who'd once been Wilson's office manager); the letter was on House of Commons headed paper; and the signature at the bottom was that of the Prime Minister. It soon emerged that the letter had been forged, and Milhench eventually served a three-month prison sentence, but press hostility continued and the Conservatives, with no justification for alleging impropriety, resorted to sanctimony, making a vague allegation of hypocrisy against Wilson because in opposition he'd been critical of property speculators. The squall subsided as quickly as it arose, but, as Joe Haines observed, it had attracted over 6,000 column inches of newsprint.

Haines was still Wilson's press secretary, with Marcia continuing to head up the political office. In the triumphant return to 10 Downing Street, Bernard Donoughue was recruited from the LSE to head a newly created policy unit. Wilson relied heavily on this trio, who were fiercely loyal and totally frank in their discussions with him. Wilson hated sycophancy, but even Haines and Donoughue winced at the brutal way Marcia sometimes spoke to their boss. But she had been with him for far longer than either of them, was a single mother struggling to keep the secret of her affair with Walter Terry, and, as her biographer Linda McDougall has revealed, was taking purple hearts to keep her awake and Valium to calm her down – a potent and dangerous combination.

In May it was announced that Marcia would go to the Lords as Baroness Falkender. Prime Ministers have often given peerages to those they work closely with. At least one has nominated their hairdresser. For Wilson to nominate his political secretary should have been uncontroversial – but this was Harold and Marcia. One of the most hostile reactions came from Joe Haines, who claimed that Wilson was simply endorsing Marcia's demand. But another of Wilson's close confidants, Barbara Castle, thought it 'astonishing how many people are outraged'. She noted in her diary how Marcia behaved 'impeccably and with dignity' when being introduced into the Lords in July 1974 (with Harold there to watch).

Such dignity was not matched by *The Times*, which chose that day to reveal the existence of her children and the name of their father.

The election was called for 10 October 1974. In the eight months since Wilson's return to power a comprehensive legislative programme had been completed or begun that was remarkable given the parliamentary arithmetic.

As mentioned, Wilson saved British lives by not engaging troops in Vietnam or Rhodesia, but he saved many more through the Health and Safety at Work Act. Introduced at a time when 1,000 people a year were killed in accidents at work, with 500,000 injured and 23 million working days lost, this much maligned legislation saw fatalities fall by 85 per cent and injuries by 77 per cent over the next 20 years.

The Race Relations Act was strengthened to give victims of discrimination tangible redress. Equal pay for women was legislated for and the sex discrimination that barred women from many jobs outlawed. The first entitlement to paid maternity leave was established, and the Advisory, Conciliation and Arbitration Service (ACAS) created to quietly go about its business of resolving disputes in the workplace.

With a slim opinion poll lead emerging, Wilson decided to go to the country. A 2.2 per cent swing from Tory to Labour gave him his fourth election victory, a record matched only by

William Ewart Gladstone in the nineteenth century. The two main parties saw their combined share of the vote fall below 75 per cent for the first time with smaller parties profiting. Notably, the discovery of oil in the North Sea helped propel the Scottish Nationalists to 11 seats. These developments combined to reduce Labour's majority to three. But they had the moral advantage of winning the popular vote, and the proliferation of seats for smaller parties made a defeat on the floor of the House less likely.

Wilson returned to No. 10 with a steely determination to keep Britain in the EEC. To succeed he knew it would be important for him to remain above the fray. This was Britain's first experience of a plebiscite, and if Parliament was subcontracting the decision to 'the people' it would be unwise for the Prime Minister to be the face of either campaign. James Callaghan, as Foreign Secretary, was deputed to achieve improvements to Britain's terms of entry in Brussels. Those negotiations were scheduled to conclude by March 1975, with campaigning commencing in May and the poll itself taking place in June.

Britain's objectives in renegotiating the terms of entry had to be realisable. Set the bar too high and clearing it would be impossible; set it too low and it would look like a cosmetic exercise, which to a large degree it was. But it wasn't meaningless. Callaghan achieved greater flexibility on the Common Agricultural Policy, an enhanced rebate of £125 million a year and, so far as protection for the Commonwealth was concerned, a huge increase in the amount of sugar that could be sold into the EEC, along with major concessions on New

Zealand dairy produce. By now, Commonwealth countries were vociferous and unanimous in their desire for Britain to remain in the Common Market.

The renegotiation was never going to conjure up unity in the Labour Party – Wilson knew that. He'd already absolved the Cabinet of collective responsibility, although they'd voted to support staying in by two to one. Ministers could choose which side they campaigned on but should avoid head-to-head confrontations. Unlike 'leave' and 'remain' in 2016, the referendum would be a yes-or-no reply to the question 'Do you think the UK should stay in the European Community (the Common Market)?' Wilson made his own position clear to Parliament in the debate over the renegotiated terms. His support for 'Yes' was all the more effective precisely because he had come to this conclusion from a position of neutrality, much as the majority of the public would do, and he maintained a low profile in the campaign.

Leaflets summarising the case for 'Yes' and 'No' were delivered to every household. The argument for 'Yes' was measured. 'Being in does not in itself solve our problems,' the leaflet proclaimed. 'No one pretends it could. It doesn't guarantee us a prosperous future. Only our own efforts will do that. But it offers the best framework for success, the best protection for our standard of living, the best foundation for greater prosperity.'

As for the 'No' leaflet, it predicted that Britain, France and Germany would cease to exist – they would become provinces of a country called Europe. Many campaigning for 'No' argued that this would be the final opportunity to pull out of the EEC – that no government would ever be foolish enough to allow Britain's membership to be reappraised in the future, when our country would be more deeply integrated.

In the referendum held on 5 June 1975, 67 per cent voted 'Yes'. All of the UK nations voted 'Yes'. Every English county voted 'Yes'. Margaret Thatcher, who'd replaced Ted Heath as Conservative leader in February, described the result as 'really thrilling'. The *Daily Telegraph* said that 'the result is quite frankly a triumph for Mr Wilson'.

Britain in the mid-1970s seemed to be a country in the midst of a nervous breakdown. Increasing militancy in the unions, supposedly influenced by Communists, brought on an attack of the Colonel Blimps. Various retired military men proclaimed their determination to defend Queen and country, if necessary by usurping parliamentary democracy. In any other decade these developments could be dismissed as the geriatric fantasies of natural Conservatives upset about Labour being back in power. But the democratically elected president of Chile, Salvador Allende, had been overthrown in 1973; Spain and Portugal were military dictatorships, and in one corner of the United Kingdom, Northern Ireland, democracy had been superseded by military force in the fight against terrorism.

General Sir Walter Walker had been Commander-in-Chief of Allied Forces in Northern Europe until his retirement in 1972. For him to call for 'dynamic, invigorating, uplifting leadership... above party politics' attracted more attention than the letters page of the *Daily Telegraph* normally would. That he should follow this up by suggesting to another paper that 'perhaps the country might choose rule by the gun in preference to anarchy' heightened interest in the volunteers he was recruiting.

Wilson, for all his level-headed pragmatism, may well have been paranoid, but he had much to be paranoid about. As we've seen, MI5 had opened a file on him in the 1940s. He knew about the attempt to murder Liberal leader Jeremy Thorpe's gay lover, Norman Scott, and, in 1975, Wilson was told that the security service had investigated a plot to remove his government in 1968. For seven years nobody had thought to tell him about it. And in 1976 there were six burglaries at the homes of close aides, and one at the Buckinghamshire country house that Wilson still owned. The South African secret service, BOSS, was certainly active in Britain, as was the KGB. As for our own security services, both MI5 and MI6 were laws unto themselves until 1989, when the first parliamentary oversight through the Intelligence and Security Committee was established. Wilson's paranoia was perhaps a little more understandable in this context.

Harold Wilson is the only post-war Prime Minister to leave office at a time of his choosing. Churchill is sometimes said to have done so, but he was 80 years of age, had suffered a stroke and, as his biographer Andrew Roberts records, felt he'd been hounded from office by MPs anxious to crown his successor. Over 50 years later, Tony Blair would know how Churchill had felt. Wilson's decision to go at around the time of his sixtieth birthday may have come as a shock to the public, but it was planned well in advance. The timing had been agreed with Mary, the Queen had been forewarned and even Roy Jenkins, hardly a confidant, reported being told several times by Wilson of this intention. While stepping down early may have once been something he wanted to do for Mary's sake, it had become increasingly important for his own well-being. His enthusiasm had faded, and his physical and mental health were declining.

It was during this period that he became friendly with his deputy press officer, Janet Hewlett-Davies. After her death in October 2023, Joe Haines revealed his suspicion that Janet, 22 years Harold's junior, had been having an affair with the Prime Minister. The basis for this was firstly that he'd seen her go upstairs to the living quarters at No. 10 one evening, and secondly that when he went to Chequers for Wilson's farewell party, the latter had asked him to allow Janet to take his usual room with a connecting door to Wilson's own. According to Haines, the next morning he noticed Wilson's slippers under her bed. Joe told one other person, Bernard Donoughue, who felt that being in Janet's company had a beneficial effect on Wilson's flagging morale at a difficult time.

Ben Pimlott mentioned Janet Hewlett-Davies in his 1992 biography of Wilson, describing her as 'a special favourite'. He quotes an unnamed civil servant's remarks about the amount of time she and the Prime Minister spent alone together in the Downing Street flat, concluding that '[Wilson] was careless of his own reputation, to put it mildly, and also of hers'.

But Sue Utting, who worked with both of them in Wilson's political office for ten years, thought the friendship was platonic. She remembers Janet as a petite, vivacious woman in pixie boots whom the office girls referred to affectionately as 'twinkle toes'. There was no attempt to be devious about the time she spent with Wilson. Janet was perfectly open about it. Sue always thought their shared love of Gilbert and Sullivan provided a more innocent explanation for the pleasure they found in each other's company.

Janet got on particularly well with Mary Wilson – so well, in fact, that when contemplating a house move the Prime Minister's wife enlisted Janet's help. The stairs at Lord North Street were making it an increasingly impractical retirement home. Janet and her husband Barry lived in Ashley Gardens, close to Westminster Cathedral, in a spacious flat with no stairs. Pimlott tells us that the two women went to view several flats in the vicinity with Mary disguised in a headscarf and slacks. It was Janet Hewlett-Davies who helped Harold and Mary find the home they would occupy for the rest of their lives.

20

HAROLD Wilson's sixtieth birthday was on 11 March 1976. At the Cabinet meeting five days later he announced his departure. The country had never known a Prime Minister to step down at the civil service retirement age: Churchill, Attlee, Eden and Douglas-Home had yet to arrive in 10 Downing Street by the age at which Wilson was departing. Wilson said nothing about this having anything to do with turning 60 because the man he wanted to succeed him, James Callaghan, was four years older. While it would amuse Wilson later to say he'd made way for an older man, he didn't want to hinder Callaghan's chances by making age a factor.

It wouldn't be until 5 April that Callaghan took charge, having defeated Michael Foot for the Labour leadership. There was suspicion that Wilson had gone to avoid an impending scandal but that scandal came as a result of his resignation rather than being its cause.

Britain's claim to some kind of democratic superiority over lesser nations has always been undermined by our appointed second chamber, the House of Lords. One of its more grotesque features is that every departing Prime Minister is given one final opportunity to bestow patronage in a resignation honours list. Wilson's was the subject of press speculation weeks before its publication because the Political Honours Scrutiny Committee, which provided a thin veil of accountability, was said to be having a problem with some of the names.

The following month, Wilson's list, inscribed originally, according to Joe Haines, on Marcia's lavender-coloured notepaper, was published. During his time as Prime Minister Wilson distributed fewer honours than many of his predecessors or successors. He'd ended the practice of awarding hereditary peerages and reduced the number of honours given automatically to civil servants. Most of the 42 names on this list were unremarkable: political allies, Mary's personal secretary, Harold's constituency agent. Ten names caused the controversy. The most prominent of these was James Goldsmith, financier and lifelong Tory who was being honoured 'for services to exports and ecology'. The Scrutiny Committee had objected to him receiving a peerage and downgraded it to a knighthood. The peerage awarded to Lithuanian businessman Joseph Kagan, whose textiles company manufactured the Gannex raincoat that had become a Wilson trademark, was unwise given that Kagan was under investigation by the Inland Revenue. (He was imprisoned for fraud in 1980.) Rudy Sternberg, also on the lavender list, was thought to be a KGB agent, but Wilson claimed he'd been told Sternberg had 'turned' and was now a double agent and so worthy of the peerage he was being awarded.

An unnamed 'former close colleague' was quoted in the press as saying that, with this list, Wilson had at one stroke damaged 'the House of Lords, the honours system, the Labour Party, the Jewish community and himself.' A hundred Labour MPs, incensed by the Goldsmith knighthood, publicly condemned the list. Tories on the floor of the House asked why Paddy, the Wilsons' Labrador, had been left out.

But the most venomous remarks were reserved for Marcia, whose own elevation as Lady Falkender had provoked such rage so recently. Joe Haines claimed that this wasn't Harold's list but Marcia's. Goldsmith was someone Wilson barely knew, Haines insisted, but he was a friend of Baroness Falkender, and had even offered her a directorship of a Goldsmith company.

Marcia retaliated. In a long letter to *The Times*, she declared the list to be Wilson's alone. Still an MP, Wilson issued a statement alleging an 'orchestrated vendetta' of denigration. As with the 'barefoot boy' episode in his early years as a minister, the observation, while accurate, simply raised the temperature. The press smelt blood. Someone who'd dealt so imperiously with the media was vulnerable and no longer protected by high office. All Wilson's supposed misdemeanours were regurgitated in an orgy of abuse.

If Wilson was guilty of anything, it was naivety. He should have known that his resignation honours carried the threat of reputational damage. He'd failed to treat it seriously enough. Haines's memoir, *The Politics of Power*, published the following year, extended and deepened the controversy.

Haines's suggestion that Marcia had dictated the list was as insulting to Wilson as it was to the woman who worked for him. As Linda McDougall points out, this all happened in an analogue age: 'People had typewriters and secretaries, and secretaries had pens and scrap paper, could do shorthand and often wrote things down while their boss peered over their shoulder. What could have been more normal than Harold Wilson and his political secretary discussing his resignation honours list together?' Marcia said that Haines disliked women and had a grudge against university graduates. 'I was both – a double offence.' Pimlott describes Haines as 'puritanical, abrasive and even misanthropic'. This explains why not everyone was convinced by his story about Hewlett-Davies and Wilson having a sexual relationship, revealed when neither Harold or Janet could respond.

Harold Wilson remained on the back benches that he'd avoided during most of his extraordinarily successful parliamentary career for seven years. His had been the first administration under which more money was spent on education than defence – so it was fitting that his final contribution in the Commons was on the subject of universities. He went to the Lords as Baron Wilson of Rievaulx. By then Alzheimer's was beginning to destroy that magnificent brain. But he kept a regular lunch appointment in the Lord's dining room every Wednesday, seated between Mary and Marcia. After he died, on 24 May 1995, aged 79, Mary and Marcia continued the arrangement – at a table for two.

During the tributes in Parliament that followed news of his death, Tony Blair, who'd yet to become only the second Labour leader to win an election since Attlee, said: 'Harold Wilson... was to politics what the Beatles were to popular culture. He simply dominated the nation's political landscape.' Others pointed out that while one of Wilson's great achievements was to hold together a fractious party, it was only one of many. His administrations improved the lives of ordinary citizens to an extraordinary degree: protecting ethnic minorities, allowing unhappy couples to divorce, legalising homosexuality, ending barbaric backstreet abortions, providing homes, and introducing statutory redundancy payments, disability rights, the concept of gender equality and the Open University. In such a long political career, he was bound to make enemies, but the charge of being underhand or devious doesn't stick, not least because such pejorative terms were mostly used by those he'd simply outsmarted.

Everyone who knew him, in whatever capacity, friend or foe, testified to his decency, utter lack of pomposity and unfailing kindness. Perhaps the most eloquent testimony to his skill as a politician came from one of his fiercest critics, the *Times* journalist Bernard Levin, who wrote: 'Harold Wilson's... mastery of the political arts was unceasingly displayed, to the confounding of the prophets, the discomfiture of his critics and the helpless rage of his political opponents.'

ACKNOWLEDGEMENTS

My thanks to George Owers at Swift Press for commissioning this book, and my agent, Clare Alexander, who was convinced I could write it in the required timescale while also completing the novel I was working on. As usual, she was right.

Mark Richards, the co-founder of Swift, became my editor when George left and helped enormously by relaxing the deadline a little. I'm also grateful to Lucie Ewin, Alex Billington and Alex Middleton for their editing expertise.

Chris Awre, one of Larkin's successors as Librarian at the University of Hull, gave me access to Wilson's two memoirs, *The Making of a Prime Minister 1916–1964* and *The Labour Government 1964–1970: A Personal Record* as well as a whole archive of Wilson material.

In writing a concise biography I'm conscious of the debt I owe to those who wrote the full-length versions which made my task possible. Chief among these were Ben Pimlott's superlative *Harold Wilson* from 1992 and the fresh perspective of *Harold Wilson: The Winner* by my former colleague on

Labour's benches in the Commons, Nick Thomas-Symonds, published in 2022.

These two books top my recommended further-reading list, but I also valued *Wilson: The Authorised Life* by Philip Ziegler, *Harold Wilson: The Authentic Portrait* by Leslie Smith and other Wilson biographies by Paul Routledge, Austen Morgan and Andrew Roth.

There is no better description of the impact that William Beveridge had on British society than *The Five Giants* by Nicholas Timmins, and for those interested in Harold Wilson's alleged paranoia about the security service, Christopher Andrew's authorised history of MI5 (*The Defence of the Realm*) is a fascinating read.

I lived through the Wilson period, but for those who didn't, reading David Kynaston's books will make you feel as though you had. I plundered *Austerity Britain*, *Family Britain*, *Modernity Britain* and *A Northern Wind* for some of the contemporary references to my subject.

To repeat a point I make in the book, there are many biographies of Harold Wilson but only one of Marcia Williams. Fortunately it was published in time for me to benefit from Linda McDougall's valuable insight. Linda's *Marcia Williams: The Life and Times of Baroness Falkender* is essential reading for anyone looking to immerse themselves further in the life of one of Britain's great Prime Ministers.

Finally, my thanks to Sue Utting, to whom this book is dedicated, and my old friend from Parliament, George Howarth. They both worked with Wilson and knew him better than most.